My Pink Rose For Katie Love

Lee Kennedy-Johnson

DWD Digital Enterprises

All Rights Reserved. This Publication Of My Pink Rose For Katie Love Shall Not Be Reproduced Or Replicated In Any Form Or By Any Means, Including Scanning, Copying, Or Otherwise. Without Prior Written Permission Of The Copyright Holder. Lee Kennedy-Johnson © 2015

Email: Leekennedyjohnson@Mypinkroseforkatielove.com

DWD Digital Enterprises retains all rights to the website.

www.mypinkroseforkatielove.com © 2023, the artwork for the cover and cover design for My Pink Rose for Katie Love, and formatting with DWD Digital Enterprises-Publishing David W. Dobbs ©2023

Email: daviddobbs@dwddigitalenterprises.com

Email: publisherdaviddobbs mypinkroseforkatielove.com

Table of Contents

1. Introduction
2. CHAPTER ONE
3. CHAPTER TWO
4. CHAPTER THREE
5. CHAPTER FOUR
6. CHAPTER FIVE
7. CHAPTER SIX
8. CHAPTER SEVEN
9. CHAPTER EIGHT
10. CHAPTER NINE
11. CHAPTER TEN
12. CHAPTER ELEVEN
13. CHAPTER TWELVE
14. CHAPTER THIRTEEN
15. CHAPTER FOURTEEN
16. CHAPTER FIFTEEN
17. CHAPTER SIXTEEN
18. CHAPTER SeVENTEEN
19. CHAPTER EIGHTEEN
20. CHAPTER NINETEEN

21. CHAPTER TWENTY
22. CHAPTER TWENTY ONE
23. CHAPTER TWENTY TWO
24. CHAPTER TWENTY THREE

1. Introduction

My Pink Rose for Katie Love, is a wonderful depiction of the love of and affection for a family canine pet-Katie Love. This story will describe most of her life and background that is based upon the actual life of Katie Love, with some additional fictional developments as expressed through multiple viewpoints-even from Katie Love herself. This story is a wonderful expression of love and affection, mystery, and many adventures of Katie Love that can only be told from the viewpoint of Katie Love, and the many people who come to know her. Her story will make you wonder about the special life of your family pet when you're not around. Enjoy the life and special adventures of Katie Love with that thought in mind.

I want to thank Barbara and Ken Evans for sharing their love of

Kate with me over the years of our friendship. It has been a joy and honor to know them, and Kate.

I would also like to dedicate this book to everyone who has supported me over the years in my writing and story telling, especially all of my children. Also to everyone who has ever had a special love for their pets, and the warmth and affection that is given by them unconditionally.

Lee Kennedy-Johnson

2. CHAPTER ONE

    The February day was cold, but the winter sun was warm where Katie Love lay cozily on a pile of fresh hay on the open side of her Tepee. The warmth of the mid-day sun made her drowsy, its rays reflecting off her long, coat of white, tangled strings of fur, as if it were embedded with diamonds. That same iridescent sunlight reflected off dewdrops on her shaggy coat, and made a hazy picture of other-worldliness, as though Katie might suddenly awaken a beautiful warrior-princess in human form. That was not Katie Love's dream, only the fancy of the Artist, that stood in the large square window of the pretty gray and white country home, seemingly studying the canvas and the sleeping canine model all at once. The leafless branches of the trees crackled in the breeze as if an alarm for Katie to shift position…and for the Artist to set aside her paintbrush and ensile, and fetch food and water for her subject…

    Katy Love woke out of her dreamy past at intervals to roll about in the hay and work her shanks and back to awaken them from their aches and stiffness. She had been dreaming of her beginning on the small farm in Pennsylvania, near Sweet Valley, a small place with winter-green Fur trees and tall Pines. A fresh water creek wound its way through Plum Creek County like a wispy ribbon cascading over rock, boulders, and gravel seen beneath the crystal clear water at its shallows. It ran through the Coats Family Farm that lies between Marshall Hollow and Shickshinny skimming through the woods and plains. There were two hundred acres of meadow grass upon the hills, and another two hundred in wheat and hay that wafted in the wind on the upper flat land of Levi Coats small sheep farm; its spread lay twenty miles south of the Village Township of Plum Creek County.

In the spring the meadows turned pale green and darkened as summer approached with splashes of wild Sunflowers, Bluebells, and gossamer Dandelions that tickled her nose as well as the flesh-pink noses of her young Masters of the humankind. She had only a brief experience in the meadows of the small farm, but the memory of the smell of it, and the tingling fear she felt back then still gave her a sense of exuberance.

She was small, only a pup, and sank down in the tall blades of meadow grass frightened that her young masters would never find her, but at her puppy yelps she was soon rescued amid a boy's laughter, and a girl's screeching cries of delight.

Katie Love was the only female of her mother's first litter of six at a mature age. She was larger than her five brothers that disappeared one after the other as soon as they were weaned, and lapping up water from a bowl, and partaking of soft nib-bits of puppy food from a shallow troth. Kate was left alone unnamed, bereft of brothers she struggled to remember, but soon forgot, as she snuggled close to her mother who nuzzled her and let her nurse of the milk still left in her pap.

Katie's dozing dreams brought her Mother into focus, the large genteel creature that cared for her so constantly, and at every strange or new sound that came into the barn her mother provided a great hiding place beneath plenty layers of white wavy hair. The humankind called her mother Shag or Shaggy, but back then in her beginnings Katie Love was called *little-girl.* It was not a name, but a reference, one that Jake Wilson, Master Coats farm hand, used frequently, and others such as *female-dog or female-sheepdog* when prospective buyers came looking. Jake would click his tongue and shake his shaved-head when the mix of farmers and ranchers from near and far, serious about their canines, would leave without taking *little-girl* with them. "You a pitiful pup, *little-girl,* hiding under your momma's fur when folks come look'n to buy your little self!" Jake stepped to the center post in the tall barn and reached for a large pair of shears that hung on a big nail. He came back across the straw-strewn floor of the barn carrying the large scissors close to his side, and let himself into the pen. Kate remembered watching as old Jake as he trimmed her mother's white coat of long slightly corded hair with its hidden gray roots. Shaggy gave a low growl of protest that Jake only chuckled to hear. "I see, you a bit upset, but Boss say to trim you up a bit, and that's what I got to do, Shag. Now you be still, or you might end up looking like those sheep of yours at a botched shearing. Might, if I could, just leave you to sheep-shearing time, get rid of this tangle, and start over…Jake laughed. Now wouldn't you be a pretty sight skin naked like those sheep you're so fond of! At Jake's smooth teasing voice Shaggy stood docile and little-girl watched as Jake cut her mother's thick layered hair-diluting her hiding places, barking as she ran at Jake in his knee-bent stoop, but he only laughed as she'd dart away and run at him again in protest. When he'd finished the trimming, as he stood, he scooped-up little-girl in his large dark hands and scratched her all over while she fought and wiggled so hard he pressed his grip.

"No wonder nobody wants to buy you, little-girl, you won't be still long enough so they get to know you – that's if you did come out a' your hidey-place! Jake's hold loosed as little-girl's sharp little teeth pierced his skin, and little-girl jumped and landed in the hay unhurt, but whimpered and barked at the unexpected decent while old Jake cursed and sucked the sting out of back of his hand. At *little-girl's* high-pitched yelps, Shag turned and barked deep and loud, nothing like little-girl's own puppy chirps, and Jake picked up his shears, and left the pen. From the other side of the fence he said "Sorry Miss Shag, but it's the truth, and you still letting her nurse like she still an infant! Spoiling her, that's what you're doing. Won't nobody buy a baby-doll wimp to tend their herds – that's for sure!" And old Jake walked out of the barn shaking his head, chuckling to himself.

Katie Love, back then, in her beginnings was a small ball of soft white downy fur, but larger than all five of her dappled brothers. Kate inherited none of the Sire's physical attributes, and all of her mother's white coloring and the agile largeness of her, a Hungarian-Komondor, whose coat never completely corded, but was tangled and wild as the ordinary working Sheepdog; not one for Kennel up-bringing with lovely cords, and accustomed to constant maintenance, attention, and training for Canine Contest; however, Shaggy was known all over Plum County for her devotion, intelligence and strength- and her natural talent for protecting the many sheep left in her care. She had fought wild dogs and a Bobcat, vicious for prey or from hunger, but most of her duty was to scare away poachers of the humankind; thieves that tried to steal away the little ones, the lambs, and sell for a profit for their tender meat, and the soft downy wool to those who weaved their own wool yarn for scarf's and infant sweaters. Shaggy had never lost a lamb or any of the sheep in her charge, so it didn't matter that her pups were half Pon, sired by a Polish Lowland Sheepdog, belonging to Levi Coats farm Manager. The Pon was little bigger than medium size, as Polish Sheepdog goes, and he was a hearty and intelligent sheepherding helper, and all the better as far as the small rancher and farmers, around Plum Creek County were concerned.

The whole valley talked about Shaggy's *miracle litter*. She was not a breed-dog, and according to the local veterinarian, she could never be. Shaggy was barren, and no need for her to be spaded. And who would have imagined that Shaggy in her matron years would be with pups? Jeff Barton, Levi Coats farm manager, was shocked, and waited a while to see if indeed it could be, and waited longer to tell his employer, working up the courage, since it was his own dear companion and sheepherder, Coty Dog that was the Sire. Levi Coats was as surprised and as shocked as Barton, but his only concern was for Shaggy's health and well-being. The vet was called and assuring he made no misdiagnoses he claimed it a miracle of nature, and everyone agreed that it was. Coty Dog's look was a mix of pride and doleful pardon, when his Master, Jeff Barton, accused him of his *deed* and praised him in the same breath. Confused he was; but was obviously very sad when Shaggy was taken from the pasture on maternity leave and housed in the big tall barn where hay and feed were stored; and that was used, when necessary, as a dispensary. Coty had been there over-night some time ago when he had a nasty nettle in his paw, and considered it a good place to be, and was comforted knowing that Shag was taken to that same good place, but he still covered his face with his paws when his Master and good friend, Jeff Barton, gazed at him with a curious account and shook his head when he couldn't seem to add things up to his satisfaction.

    Yes, Katie Love's birth home was miles and years away except in her day- dreaming, and it was only recently that she had begun to think, to recall such memories in sometimes fuzzy vision, and other times in vivid dreams. She and her five dark-haired little brothers had been born and lived in the wide, high barn in a fenced section spread with sweet smelling hay. The rest of the barn was stacked high with bundles and blocks of hay, and heavy sacks of feed that lined the long low shelves that ran the length of one side of the barn. When her siblings were no longer with her, she still had the comfort of her mother, and the barn kittens for friends. She frolicked and played with the little barn cats that dared to jump into her pen, after creeping along the fence for some time, to determine how they would be received. There were tennis balls to paw at and dig out of the hay, that the little master's had tossed in the pen, which the kittens were expert at getting up into the air, but too large for *little-girl* to catch in her mouth. Life was good. She was loved and nourished, and the little master's came to visit her, and Shaggy. And then, later they took her out of the pen to the yard to play and into the great meadows on bright sunny days.

    It was not long after old Jake's visit with the big shears that her mother was gone to tend sheep with the hired men and Coty Dog. Shaggy knew it was time, and refused to let little-girl nurse any longer, but Katie wasn't much disappointed, as she recalled, because there was only drops left of her mother's milk, and she liked the soft, chewy puppy food the humankind supplied, but she was lured by the meaty aroma of her mother's food, and often tried to sneak a taste only to be pushed away by Shaggy's big paw or warned away with a slow, quiet growl, that sent her waddling back to her own nibble's.

    Little-girl saw very little of Shaggy after she had returned to work. Shag never herded the flock, but moved like one of the sheep from pasture to pasture as their body-guard, a fearless centurion of her charges, and of the humankind to whom she belonged and loved. She had cleaned her pup, little-girl, very thoroughly; licking her with a very moist tongue, and kept her ever so close and nuzzled the last days they were to be together in the big barn, sensing their soon parting. Shag was anxious to be out under the sky with the sheep again, but she would miss her first born pup, and the last of her litter to be with her for so long a time. She scared away the barn cats, and hid the balls under the hay, so that she could have little-girl all to herself for she might never see her again...And a too wet *little-girl* from her mother's long and through bathing was not enjoying all the attention Shag was lavishing on her, but she fell asleep that night a happy pup listening to the beat of her mother's heart.

For pity little-girl was given a warm cozy bed in the mudroom of the tall old farmhouse. She was a well loved pup, but she still whined and sometimes whimpered for her mother, Shaggy. But the little masters were always at hand to pet and cuddle her out of her misery, and offered her tasty puppy treats to ease her loneness, all the while old Jake Wilson shaking his head, and warning of the spoiling of a would-be fine sheepdog when he caught the children cuddling her, or constantly carrying her about as if she were *human*.

Ω

"Can't we keep her?" Emma and Theo begged, Levi... "Shaggy will be too old to watch after the sheep and you will need her Dad." Theo begged in his negotiations to keep *little-girl* and give her a name. "We may not be keeping sheep much longer, Levi explained. I'm much too busy with the Sports Shop in Scranton, and your mother wants to open some sort of boutique in the Village." "Well then we must keep her for a pet!" Emma explained. "Why sure, and she'd double as our guard-dog!" Theo added, sure they'd won by logic.

"Despite what Jake Wilson says; *little-girl* is a working-dog. Levi explained. It's in her blood, and she will never be *just* a pet, she wouldn't be happy..." Levi sighed, not sure his argument was as good as his children's sensible logic, but things were changing and they had to change with them.

"But nobody will love *little-girl* like we do!" Emma cried, swiping at the tears spilling out her blue eyes, with the back of her hand as if they were getting in her way.

"Are we leaving the farm...?" Theo, who was almost ten years old asked, his focus suddenly changed. He waited impatiently to hear the answer while his father was *babying* his little sister. Finally he said, "Are we Dad?

"No Theo, certainly not. We will just raise the hay, and some produce. Plum Creek Farm and The Township will always be our home, unless you and Emma decide different when your mother and I turn it over to you ...when you're older..."

"What's the big pow-wow all about?" Janice Coats asked cheerfully. She'd come in from shopping in the Village, and heard, from the living room, bits of their conversation as she put away groceries in the kitchen. When she saw Emma's tearful face she chewed her bottom lip in concern, and her usually good natured Theodor looked thoroughly angry.

"The pow-wow is about the bow-wow...the pup." Levi said rubbing his short neat beard. Though Levi tried to keep the subject light, Janice could see the hurt in his blue eyes that his children were so upset. He had six-year old Emma on his knees, her eyes the same blue as her father's, and her hair as fair. Theo, so much like his mother stood in the center of the room, his arms crossed as was her habit when she was holding her temper or standing her ground. He had her russet hair, and brown eyes, but his father's lean, strong built, and the same confident stride when he walked. She laid her hand on Theo's shoulder and gave it a little squeeze. "Can't be all that bad...little-girl's not sick is she?" Janice inquired of her children.

"Daddy wont' let us keep little-girl and give her a name!" Emma exclaimed.

"Everything's changing..." Theo croaked fighting off tears.

"Oh Levi, have you told them of our plans in your...Your *only* way?" Janice sighed.

"If you mean blunt – not exactly..." Levi said avoiding his wife's scrutiny.

"Listen; my Sweets" Janice said pulling Theo down to sit next to her on the couch. "You each can pick out your very own puppy at the Shelter. I just spoke to Mrs. Willis at the Market, and she was telling me of a new batch of puppy someone's left at the shelter...you and Emma can have your pick...only a smaller breed than little-girl...that will be easier to care for, and to keep indoors, which I know you both want."

"Do I have a say in this?" Levi asked as he mopped Emma's face with his handkerchief, and cleaned her nose.

"No." Janice replied, but offered him a large and endearing smile.

"Well, I was only going to say that if they didn't like any of Mrs. Willis puppy's they could check out the Pet Stores in Scranton, tomorrow, when we go to pick up your Irish *Uncle*." Levi said and narrowed his eyes at his pretty and independent Irish wife.

"Joe! I d' almost forgotten he's coming for a visit!" Janice exclaimed. "I promised him a Sheppard's Pie and a Gooseberry Cobbler for supper tomorrow, better check the pantry..."

"Well we don't want no old store-bought puppy, we want little-girl!" Emma cried and jump off her daddy's lap. Little-girl's the best puppy in the whole world!"

"Didn't daddy explain that little-girl will want to protect the sheep just like her mother, darling? She'll be very unhappy if she can't do what she's born to do...You wouldn't want little-girl to be unhappy would you darling?"

"Nooo, Momma." Emma sniffed.

"Well let's give daddy- and little-girl a break, ok? The change will be hard for the both of them too. You see, Sometimes we have let go of those we love...let them do what they are meant to do."

"I won't ever let go of daddy!" Emma protested.

"Oh but you will..." Levi said, about ten years from now, you will think I'm the dumbest..."

"Levi…darling…!" Janice proclaimed to stop him from a pre-adolescent proverb. Looking up at Janice who was rising from the couch and Theo following Levi simply nodded his head.

"Everything will be all right guys…I promise." Levi smiled brightly. Janice heart still did that funny thing when Levi smiled so disarmingly.

"We know Dad." Theo spoke up; sorry he'd given his Dad a moment's grief. "We can check out the store-bought, can't we Em." Theo stated firmly giving Emma his big-brother stare which meant she'd better follow his lead –*if she knows what's good for her!*"

"Yeah, sure." Emma managed. "I'm going to play with little-girl…" She said and ran out of the room. "I'm sure glad Uncle Joe's coming to see us tomorrow!" She yelled cheerfully.

"Me too", Theo said. "Guess I'll go hang with Emma and little-girl." He shrugged dissatisfied with the failed negotiations and the turn of events in their lives, yet secure in his parents love.

"Well I'm glad everyone's happy about Joe's visit, Janice said urging Levi out of his favorite chair with a helping hand.

"Can't argue with that, your uncle is always a kick to have around." Levi faked a grunt having help out of his easy chair, and Janice rolled her eyes. Then seriously she said; "I just wish Judith would come with him. She's such a lovely girl, but so…strange in ways." Janice said with sincere concern.

"Well it's too long a drive for Joe, and Judith has a phobia of flying". Levi replied in his practical way. "We should plan a trip to visit them in Missouri, the kids might enjoy it since Joe and Judith lives only a few miles from Branson." Levi suggested.

"Great Idea, but don't hint at an invitation, since we've never gotten one before from Joe or Judith, but just say we're planning a trip for the kids to Branson…and take it from there."

"Why is it you're always guiding me away from my straight forward approach, my dearest…" Levi said and pulled Judith into his arms…

"Well you've never been the most subtle guy in the state…"

"That's because when I know what I want I go after it…" Levi kissed his wife and led her in a few dance steps into the kitchen... "I never would have lassoed a gal like you by the subtle approach...you had too many ahead of me...bigger, better looking guys..."

"Auh, well I don't know how I noticed a six-footer, string bean, the likes of you, showing up everywhere with that grin..." They laughed, and Levi twirled her out and swatted her fanny playfully. "What's for dinner woman? I'm starved!" He grabbing his chef's apron off a peg on the pantry door, as Janice, finger on chin and squinted eye, thought of the New York steaks she'd just bought at the local meat market knowing Levi would prefer them to the Sheppard Pie she would prepare for her Irish *Uncle,* Joe Spangle, on Sunday. If he had steak this evening, he'd be more inclined to be gracious to the Irish Sunday evening, rather than an attempt to drag them all to the Village Steak House or The Fish Fry Café near the river.

Levi was Janice's prep Chef. He'd sliced and diced with the best of them having worked at a large restaurant in Philadelphia during his four years of college at *Pennsylvania* State. Now he worked at the Island of his kitchen, in the apron and chef's hat, (Janice had given to him as a wedding present, a sentimental endearment), while Janice seared steaks on the grill and a couple of hamburgers for the kids, who were not into to steaks – yet, they so informed. Janice had flipped on the small stereo tucked in a nook in the kitchen and a voice from the past belted out "She's Always a Woman."

"You can say that again, dude!" Levi said wiggling his eyebrows comically, in a sense of the ridiculous, which always lightened their small but serious family storms involving their children.

"What else would I be, dude?" Janice teased, as she turned Steaks on the grill.

"Salad's up, love, I'm tossing plates on the table and yelling for the kids." Levi said, untying his Chef's apron and tossing his tall white hat, he ringed it on the hook.

"Better check on them, make sure they wash up before coming to supper." Janice advised.

"Re-directed as usual. I wonder if anybody believed that old Show...." Levi mumbled.

"What's that love?" Janice said flipping burgers.

"The one where Father Knows Best." Levi grumbled as he headed for the Mudroom.

3. CHAPTER TWO

Joseph Andrew Spangle, a tall muscular, rugged looking man, partly because of his scrubby growth of beard, and the inherited high cheekbones and gray eyes of his Cherokee Indian grandmother; but more so, because of his military special forces training and combat experience in Afghanistan. He had always been called *Storm Cloud,* when he was a boy; because of the Paleface side of the family claimed his eyes were colorless and sad. He had more of the Cherokee look about him, but a joyful spirit that was all his own, and still a slight Irish brogue he'd picked up from the elder Irish of his family. He thought his cousin, Janice, had gotten the best of both sides of their family; a spirited girl, but with the calm and thoughtfulness of the Cherokee. They were only eight years apart in age since his father, being the eldest son of the Spangle's married late in his life to a younger woman. His father's younger sister, Emma Mae, Janice mother, married young and had only Janice…thus they both were an only child in an Irish Catholic family that celebrated the large, noisy family that originated in the Oklahoma hill country. He and Janice were considered the oddities of an otherwise *normal* Irish Clan. And the fact that he was always "Uncle" to Janice though they were cousins, something his Aunt Emma Mae Kent, preferred for her own reasons made them double the family spectacles.

Marriage brought Joe Spangle to Missouri, and his aunt's marriage to an easterner, James Kent, which made Janice a Pennsylvania girl by birth. Janice married a fine Pennsylvania guy, she'd met at college, Levi Coats, more French than British, but a guy Joe loved and respected. And it was their two great kids, Theo and Emma, which Joe envied; since he and his wife Judith were not blessed with little ones. Joe Spangle was boot-kicking happy that Levi bought into his business and opened a franchise store in

Scranton. Levi sold hardware in Plum Creek, and sports shoes and equipment in Scranton. The guy's master's in business helped Joe over more than a few rough spots when he'd first jumped in to the business in Branson. Now he had a chain of five stores in different states, and had made Levi Coats the business head of them all in partnership. Levi Coats was Vice President of Spangle's Sport Shops. Levi conducted all out of state business by Internet, and phone, but Joe was the 'on sight guy', that took a look and measure in person - usually every three months at his chain across the Midwest. Levi was owner of his store, with rights to the Spangle name and particular products and Joe met with Levi every three or months on business, but not always for overnight or weekend visits.

Joe was pumped more about his visit with his favorite people than the business, and his face lit up when he saw the four of them waving and smiling, as he landed his Cessna, at the small private Airport just outside of Scranton. The youngsters holding a handmade 'Welcome' sign, and Emma's inability to stand still when she was excited, touched his heart and made him laugh. The weary thoughts of his troubled, temperamental wife, Judith, fled from his mind at the sight of his cousin's children. Joe's long strides across the tarmac become a full fledged jog to greet his favorite cousin and her family. The title "Uncle" felt very good to him as he was so loudly greeted by the children. Joe laughed at Emma's bouncing like a pogo-stick and yelling "Uncle Joe! Uncle Joe!" He managed to swoosh her up in his arms while Theo grabbed hold at his elbow, grinning like a banshee. "What are you guys feeding these two little apes?" Joe teased as he greeted Janice and Levi. "Sugar; Sugar." Janice laughed, and tip-toed for his kiss, while Levi pounded his back.

It was a chattering reunion, mostly Theo and Emma exclaiming over the puppy they had, but couldn't keep and checking out "store puppies"...but none could ever be as good as the one they had at home...they explained, their words running over each others, their mix of heartache and excitement making their eyes large and moist. Joe told them that he had a store bought dog once and it was the best dog he'd ever had...and the only one, but Joe didn't mention that fact. So Janice and the children took tour of the Pet Stores while Levi and Joe took care of business at the store. They all had a drive-through breakfast, and Levi and Joe promised Janice that they would be finished with business at one for a sit-down lunch at the Harvest Restaurant. They were thirty minutes late.

Their day was filled with a variety of necessary business for the Spangle Sport's Store, home and farm, but included plenty of fun for Emma and Theo, who enjoyed the Pet Store tour, but it was obvious to Janice their heart was not ready to choose a replacement for *little-girl,* and Janice would not force the issue. *In time,* she mused to herself while they waited for Levi and Joe at the Harvest Restaurant.

After a hardy meal it was to the Arcade Video Game Room for vicious competition with Joe and Levi acting like boys in a challenge with Theo and Emma, and gaining looks of both approval and envy from the kids and teens nearby. Janice felt a stab of sympathy for kids who lacked a *real* relationship with their parents and vice-versa. Next was a hilarious comedy performance by a local theater group, called 'Chocolate Chips', and following came 'The Cowboys', a loud rock and roll band – Country Style, which had the rather taciturn, conservative, Uncle Joe Spangle shifting his boots around at the downtown –town square. Janice and Levi egged him on with rhythmic clapping and a bit of sing-a-long that encouraged the rest of the crowd to join in. Theo and Emma only looked at each other and shrugged, but when the *real* rock and roll band took the stage so did the kids, Theo and Emma leading the pack. Pre-school to teen- all were making their moves, most, very gymnastically, others in very rhythmic *bone-antics* to the beating of the drums and electrified stringed instruments, which had the crowd ecstatic. They left as the soothing sounds of the Jazz Band quieted the crowd and sent everyone home with the laid-back tones of the clarinet, the Base, and the easy cascading of piano keys.

Emma fell asleep as soon as Levi accessed the highway in

the family SUV and headed home to Plum Creek. Janice offered Joe to 'ride shotgun' in the front passenger's seat, but he climbed into the back with the kids. "You might be sorry, Joe." Janice whispered. But Joe waved away her caution.

Joe Spangle's heart was full as he glanced over a marketing presentation, the daylight dimming as the miles were left behind on the Highway 120 and on to the less formal route 80. He dropped the folder on the floorboard, when he felt the simultaneous leaning of Emma and Theo on either side of him, which fixed him, immoveable between them.

"Are you ok back there, Joe?" Janice said twisting in her seat for a view of them. "I tried to warn you..." She said at the sight of her two happy, exhausted kids asleep on the lean.

"Fine. Fine, Joe grinned. "I'm the cream in the Oreo."

Theo and Emma were jostled awake when Levi served to miss the wide flatbed two-ton truck charging down the middle of the road at breakneck speed, stirring up the dust and gravel on the country road, and laying heavy on the horn. The kids, undisturbed, woke-up with sandman eyes and croaked, "Are we home yet?"

Who the heck drives like that?" Joe exclaimed, checking over Emma and Theo patting them as if they might have suffered trauma.

"That's Clever Stevens...Lives couple miles from our place." Levi informed, unable to control the anger in his voice as he smoothed their ride.

"Levi has talked to Clever about his driving, but without any improvement on Clever's part, as you've seen just now." Janice said with a audio sigh.

"Someone even had the Sheriff come out to set the old guy straight, but no results." Levi interjected.

"Couple nights in jail might make for improvement." Joe offered.

"Well something has to be done before he kills somebody!" Levi said.

"Maybe he just needs glasses." Theo yawned.

"Recon it could be as simple as that?" Joe chuckled.

The last few miles home Emma and Theo were wide awake and complaining of hunger, but as soon as the car stopped in their driveway they pressed out of their seat belt and ran toward the back of the house. "Come on Theo, hurry-up!" Emma called dashing ahead of her brother. "We got 'a check on *little-girl!* "Bet she missed us something awful!"

"That's the puppy they told you about." Janice said as she relayed shopping bags to Joe that Levi was swiftly handing out to her out of the back of the SUV. Levi held a box of various supplies on his shoulder and pushed the hatch-door -shut.

"Yeah they're crazy about that pup!" Levi said as the three of them, with their burden, headed for the front door with the day's loot.

"Well I know the feeling – or have known…you remember Roscoe, Janice? Joe asked.

"Oh sure, how could I forget? You certainly had plenty of *feeling* for that pup!" Janice chuckled.

"That bad?" Joe grinned as they entered the house at its entry hallway.

"Why you wouldn't speak to anyone until Roscoe was half grown!" Janice exaggerated

"Oh, come now Jan." Joe said soberly.

"Well that's what Uncle Joe-Senior said; and your mom… Aunt Koki said she had fought with Uncle Joe so that you could bring Roscoe with you to visit us." Janice summarized the memory.

"Car trip?" Levi asked as they put up the supplies in the kitchen pantry.

"Only way to travel as far as my Dad was concerned." Joe chuckled. "Actually it wasn't so bad. Roscoe was a pretty decent fellow. Only thing Dad objected to was Roscoe's persistent paws on the back of the driver's seat and with every braking turn, Roscoe would bark like crazy! Finally Dad yelled, "Joseph Andrew would you do something with that *blankity-blank* backseat driver!" They all three laughed at the story, and Joe said "I sure miss the old man...he's been ...gone...died five years ago, but I still miss the old dude."

"Me to, Joe." Janice said and gave her cousin's arm a quick squeeze of sympathy. "I'm glad Koki is doing well...I know she loved your dad like crazy." Janice added and Joe gave a smiling nod of agreement.

The adults were in the kitchen just finishing stocking the pantry; and Janice assuring Joe that she had all the makings for the Shepherd's Pie and Gooseberry Cobbler, he craved, for Sunday Supper when Emma burst into the room with Theo following at her heels.

"How hungry are you guys?" Janice inquired as she signaled a bit of decorum, to her children. They all shrugged. "Well you can't be very hungry with that response." Janice said. "Soup and sans then," she smiled and got out the soup pot. With home-grown and home-canned Mason jar vegetable's and Beef Broth Janice had the royal blue iron pot of soup ready to serve in no time. Levi was putting deli meant sandwiches together with a divided dish of condiments to choose from. "To each his own." Levi said as he placed the platter on the table, and then glanced up at his two children who stood near the table; Theo, the serious one, the strength of a man growing in his character all ready, and Emma, the light brown haired one with freckles across her nose, who was full of heart and emotion for those she loved. What a wonder they were, these children he'd been blessed with Levi mused as he smiled at the two silent ones waiting to be heard.

"What's on your mind?" Levi asked. "I can see something is – it's *all over* you both." Levi said, and waited. "We want to bring little-girl to show Uncle Joe how cool she is." Theo said. At that Janice turned an expression of refusal already forming on her pretty face. Joe could hardly resist the hopeful strain in the children's faces.

"I don't think Joe would be interested in the pup, besides he's got on his good clothes, and wouldn't wish to have them smell like dog, I'm sure." Janice insisted.

"I wouldn't mind, with your permission, of course." Joe

added, and nodded at Janice, not to infringe on a mother's authority.

"You're a wise man, Joe." Levi half whispered as he handed Joe a cold bottle of beer.

"Then may we, Mommy? Pleaeeeeese!" Emma begged.
"I suppose so." Janice sighed and pulled open the drawer of the Buffet and handed Joe a faded tablecloth. "Do put this across your lap to protect your clothes Joe..." Janice advised as Theo and Emma dashed to the mudroom to fetch little-girl.

"Oh I don't think that's necessary, Jan. I'll just pet her where she stands..." Joe replied. And then the children rushed in with a ball of white fur. "You want 'a hold her Uncle Joe?" Emma beamed, and Joe quickly shook the tablecloth from its fold and laid it over his lap.

Joe found *little- girl* very delightful and little-girl responded in kind. She'd never felt this way about any adult humankind, her heart was strictly open to the little masters, Theo and Emma.

"I think its puppy-love!" Levi laughed stroking his beard. And Joe cuddling her close said, "Tell me you haven't a buyer for this one Levi" Joe Spangle exclaimed in his slightly Irish brogue. Janice and Levi exchanged knowing looks, both aware that Joe was thoroughly naive as to little-girls breed. Levi was willing to let Joe find out for himself, but Janice pierced him with her eyes for her husband to come *clean.*

"Uh, Joe, I guess you realize that this particular puppy will soon get as big as a house?"

"Oh, Levi, for goodness sake!" Janice said placing the lid on the soup pot and facing them at the table. "Joe, dear, she began, the puppy will grow-up to a very large dog, but Levi is exaggerating a bit. Little-girl is a Komondor, a body-guard for sheep, it's in her bloodline to protect the flock or herd she's assigned to, and Komondor's are also very protective of their owners and their family and friends. Perhaps you'd like to meet the puppy's mother, Shaggy, before you make up your mind about *little-girl*?" Janice soulfully advised.

"Well, as usual, when you're visiting with us, Shaggy is out across the way with the sheep, Joe. But Jeff Barton will have them back in the near pasture tomorrow and you can meet the Mom before you leave tomorrow. "Well sure, if I'm still here, but I've made up my mind about this one." Joe said.

"Joe, the puppy won't be an indoor pet for long, and Komondor's love to be outdoors, they like to roam when they are not standing guard, like a Centurion, over their flock of sheep...and their maintenance, if you want them indoors, quiet challenging..." Janice explained.

"Well I have six hundred acres for her to roam in, and when I'm away from home it would be great to have a large centurion looking after Judith and my Aunt Mattie, who lives with us –She's the chief cook and bottle washer around the house."

"Well as long as you know what you're getting into Joe, the Pup is yours, Levi said. She is my gift to you." Levi chuckled and offered his hand for Joe's agreement.

"You've got a deal my friend." Joe said clasping hold of Levi's hand firmly. "We both agree then that she's priceless, right?" Joe said.

"Whatever floats you boat, ole' pal." Levi laughed.

4. CHAPTER THREE

Sunday morning dawned bright, but by early afternoon the sky became drab with gray on gray; gray sky, gray clouds. Joe Spangle cell- phoned for flight information as he studied the sky and was instructed to leave early in order to miss the impending stormy weather heading for eastern states. His disappointment showed plainly on his rugged face when he told Janice and Levi the news as he stepped back inside the house and into the living room.

"Oh, Joe, dinner won't be ready for an hour...I'm so sorry!" Janice exclaimed.

"It is I that is sorry to miss such an old Irish delight, and that you've gone to such trouble to prepare my Sheppard's pie and Gooseberry cobbler...love." Joe kissed Janice on the forehead. "I am sorry Jan." He said and hugged her close.

"When do you need to leave, Joe?" Levi asked.

"The sooner the better. I'll gather up my stuff...and little-girl..." Theo stood by disappointment apparent in his brown eyes. He lifted his ball cap and turned it forward on his dark hair pulling down the bill to shield his watery eyes. "I'll tell Emma, she's with little-girl." Theo said as he turned away. "Theo, please bring the tote, and the puppy's blanket...I'll sack up her food and treats... Don't forget her teething bone..." Janice added.

"I got it covered Mom." Theo called back, as he hurried toward the mudroom.

"That's my boy!" Levi said quietly, proud of his son, and then to Joe; "I'll bring the car around front." He said dreading the emotional parting- not only of Joe Spangle, but of Emma and Theo's farewell to their beloved pup, little-girl.

"Dad says you have a farm too, Uncle Joe. Will little-girl take care of your sheep when she's older?" Theo asked as he sat the puppy tote at Joe's feet where he sat on the sofa; his luggage set on the floor beside him.

"I don't have sheep, Theo, just a few cows I raise for the Dairy Farmers; perhaps little…uh girl can help keep my cows in line." Joe smiled. But if not, I will enjoy her company."

"That's good, because Jake, Dad's helper, says little girl is spoiled for work, but her five little brothers' were sold to farmers soon as they were weaned."

"Well I think little-girl can do just about anything she set her mind to." Joe replied with a grin. And Janice returned from the kitchen with a bag of puppy food and a bottle of water, said: "Levi does not agree with Jake's dire prophecy he has of your pup Joe. "I'm sure little-girl will make a fine helper for your herd, and it will be good for her. I hope you utilize all her talents, Joe." Janice concluded.

"I'll do my best; you all can count on that." Joe smiled, and stood as he looked around for Emma. She came slowly into the room with little-girl, a big bundle for a small girl; tears spilling form her blue eyes. Joe felt the wince in his chest, his heart moved by her tears. He stooped, leaning on his heels as Emma gave little-girl over to him. "You have to name her Uncle Joe…She's yours now and you got to give her a *real* name!" Emma exclaimed.

"You're so right, Emma, and I've been thinking I'd like to call her *Kate.* It's a good old Irish name, and I like it. How 'bout you?"

"It's per…perfect…" Emma hiccupped, but she couldn't stop the well of tears. Joe handed Kate to Theo and took Emma in his arms and stood up. "Now listen here, little Miss, you got a stop this bawling 'because you're breaking my heart…"

"I'll miss you too a whole bunch Uncle Joe!" Emma cried and wiped at her eyes.

"Well I'll be back and we can visit on Skype; Me and Kate with you and Theo. How does that sound?"

"Sounds good…" Emma hiccupped.

"Well all right, then. Let's say we have a date next Friday, then?"

"Fine…" Emma sniffed.

"Emma, Uncle Joe has to leave so he can fly home before the storm…" Janice said and held out her arms to Emma. Emma clung to Janice a moment and when she was ready to face the enviable after her mother's encouragement she was let down on her own feet. Levi came in from outdoors and said, "Jeff Barton has Shaggy down from the pasture if you want to take a look at the pup's momma, Joe."

"Sure." Joe grinned, and gathered up his tote and slung his suit-bag over his shoulder while the others carried Kate and her luggage out to the SUV.

"Daddy, Uncle Joe named little-girl Kate!" Emma exclaimed.

"Well that's a fine name for a fine pup, Emma." Levi smiled at *his* 'little girl' with her tear-stained face, her happiness and heartbreak showing in her shinning blue eyes. Levi made himself a promise to take Emma and Theo to find their own puppy as soon as they were willing.

The newly named puppy, Kate, wiggled out of Theo's arms and hit the ground running at the sight of Shaggy, and the canine mother breaking speed at the sight of her pup. "This is not a good idea" Janice said, to Levi as he loaded the back of the SUV. "It will be all right, Hon, don't worry so much." Levi said and put his arm around her waist as they stood watching the reunion, and Joe's face at the sight of what Kate would look like in a few months time. Joe glanced at Janice, and she gave a little nod of her head with a slight grimace. "I know, I know, Joe sighed, you tried to warn me…" And at that Shaggy followed Kate to Joe Spangle and took to Joe as quickly as her pup had. Shaggy sniffed at him, and gave her approval with an open smile, and her tail whipping a breeze. But then when she realized that her pup was leaving with the tall humankind, Shaggy began to protest barking loud as she followed the SUV out of the driveway.

"Shaggy come back!" Theo and Emma yelled as they ran after Shaggy, and Janice and Jeff Barton followed the kids in an easy jog. "She'll stop and come back on her own." Jeff Barton told

Janice.

"Theo! Emma!" Janice called. " Wait!" The four of them stood at the end of the driveway, and as surely as Jeff Barton had said, Shaggy stopped as soon as the SUV rounded the curve and was out of sight. She stood staring after it, but at the sudden sound of thunder Shaggy turned and came running home. The thunder rolled and roared as Shaggy kept up her pace when the big wide-bed truck came speeding down the road behind her, weaving over the road erratically, from one side to the other, completely out of control. "Oh God help us it's Clever Stevens!" Janice exclaimed. Jeff Barton grabbed Emma up into his arms and Janice took Theo's hand and they ran and stood behind the brick pillar that held their mailbox, only to witness the big truck zigzagging crazily. It hit Shaggy with its big tires and the impact sent her airborne into the grass beside the dusty road. Emma and Theo screamed, and Janice clamped her hand over her mouth to stay the shock and hysteria she felt. Jeff Barton ran to Shaggy even though he knew there was no saving her. Janice held Theo back from following Jeff, shaking her head in sadness and shock, and trying to comfort Emma who was in her arms clinging and wailing as she took her children back across the wide yard and into the safety of their home.

When Jeff Barton came to the house, Janice called for him to come in as she was transfixed with comforting Emma and Theo. "I could kill that stupid Clever Stevens!" Theo spat out as Jeff Barton entered the room with his hat in hand and his eyes red from the burning of unshed tears. Theo knew that Shaggy had not survived as soon as he saw Jeff's face, and Janice couldn't find her voice to dissuade her son of his wrath, her own anger kindled and ready to explode. She'd speak about it another time, and soon.

"I'm so ...so sorry Mrs. Coats, kids...I never should have brought Shaggy down to the house like I did...should have had her on a leash...just never occurred to me that..." Jeff Barton could say no more as his emotions seemed to cut off his ability to speak. He dropped his head.

"Mr. Barton it was not your fault!" Judith exclaimed quietly and firmly. It's all the fault of that Clever Stevens." It's a wonder he's not killed any one of us the way he drives, and the county seems helpless to do anything to stop him!"

"Well they will now, I'll see to it." Jeff replied. "I've called the Sheriff's office, and officers are on their way…The Vet, Doc Sawyers, is on his way – not that there is anything he can do, but just make an official report to the officers when they get here. Are you up to talking to the county police when they get here Mrs. Coats?" Jeff Barton concluded.

"Yes, I'll be all right, and thank you, Mr. Barton. Just send the officers' up to house when they arrive, and will you take care of the business with the Vet…and…well…Shag…" Janice tried not to say more than necessary for fear of upsetting her children even more.

"Don't worry Miss, I can take care of things, just don't you and the children upset yourselves any more…"

"Thank you…" Janice replied and turned her focus on her children.

Ω

"Good grief, I'm beginning to doubt if we've done the right thing for the kids, and for this pup, Levi!" Joe Spangle exclaimed at all the commotion going on at his and Kate's departure. The children were upset, the pup's mother was chasing after them barking as if they were thieves escaping with a treasure…which they were…hers, and Theo and Emma's. Joe felt like he'd betrayed them all. "Maybe we should turn around and take Kate back…"

"Well I can't accuse you of buyer's remorse now can I?" Levi said glancing at Joe."

"Yeah, well the *priceless pup* doesn't sound too happy about the whole thing either." Joe said nodding toward the backseat where Kate was *squirreling* around in her tote and yapping in her high-pitched crying.

"Shaggy will turn back home, it's just her last goodbye to her baby. We can't hold that against her." Levi said.

"Guess not or the kids for that matter…It's hard for them as well." Joe concluded.

"That's true, but I promise you they will soon be enthralled about the puppies, they will pick out and claim for their very own in a few days, and their pain will soon be forgotten; especially since they know Kate is with someone who loves her as much as they do – and Shag has her own sense of that too…I guarantee it." Levi said. "Lighten up, man!" He added.

"You sure have a handle on stuff like this dude." Joe said shaking his head. I guess that's what makes you so darn good at what you do for the business, the stores." Joe remarked, as he tuned in the passenger's seat and gave Kate a piece of Beef Jerky he found in his jacket pocket, which was an immediate pacifier. "You seem to have everything figured out beforehand…" Joe went on.

"I have plenty of good heads, including yours, to help me, and the key word is *seems*. I don't always have an answer…"Levi replied.

"Could've fooled me…" Joe said and tossed his leather jacket in the backseat, which landed next to Kate's tote and set her nose to the business of sniffing it out. Joe twisted in the passenger seat and stared out the back window of the SUV into the gray afternoon. There was no Miss Shaggy following, and the sound of rolling thunder gave concern for a cancelled flight. He'd flown in the worst kinds of weather on Special Forces assignments for the Military, but it was different in the States, and with small private Airports. Caution and safety was their mainstay, and Joe prepared for the possibility of an overnight stay at a motel in Scranton, but the closer they came to Scranton the lighter the sky, and he was glad, and hoped that Levi would not be driving home to a storm…

"Hey Joe, Levi said as they neared the Airport, Janice and I have been talking about taking the kids to Branson this Summer… would you and Judith like to join us there?"

"Uh, well, sure, Levi. Yeah, that would be great! Joe said. Levi glanced at Joe as he parked the car. Joe's enthusiasm sounded a little strained and he caught Joe's arm as he loosed the seat belt. "Wait a minute Joe. Look I didn't mean to put you on the spot. I just wanted you to know we'll be in town this summer – if you and Judith would like to join us …"

"Actually I would love it." Joe heaved a sigh and gazed out the window at the sun breaking through gray clouds. "Look, man, I don't like to talk about my wife…she's a lovely woman, a good woman, but she…well she has a lot of hang-ups…I never know what she is going to do or how she will act from one day to the next…It's hard to explain…and I would not want her to hurt or offend you or Janice and certainly not the kids…" Judith can be very…uh… unkind" Joe said unable to say *cruel- with her words.* He owed her some kind of protection.

"Well don't worry about it, Joe. We'll just let you know when we're in town, and play it by ear from there." Levi told him.

"That's probably the best way; but believe me I'd love for you guys to stay with us at the farm, I know Mattie would love it, but I can't speak for Judith."

"I understand. Come on let's have you and Miss Kate on your way, I've held you up long enough." Levi said.

"It's been a blast! – A homey kind of blast – if you know what I mean." Joe laughed. Thanks a mil' Levi." Joe said as they headed for the Cessna after he registered his fight plan at the office. "Anytime, Joe. You're always welcome – and Judith too when she's able…" Levi gave Joe a hand shake and a sound pat on his back and said goodbye and God's speed. Levi stayed and watched Joe taxi the small plane and when he got clearance he set out down the length of the port runway and into the sky. Levi drove home more aware of and more thankful for the healthy wife he had…and felt a deep pity for Joe Spangle for it was obvious he loved his wife very much.

5. CHAPTER FOUR

    Clever Stevens finished the last of the Fifths of Jack Daniels he had stockpiled beneath the seat of his fifteen year-old wide-bed truck. He was parked in back of a grove of trees along County Road 10 where he had hid when he saw his wife's jeep coming towards him in the distance. The woman had a mouth on her, and he was in no mood to listen to her put-downs and complaints. She could be real sweet at times, but those times were a long stretch apart, and he hadn't the patience to wait for her sugar and spice to show up. He was just going to take a couple of sips of *the good stuff* to see him through whatever it was he was about to go through when Kelly Sue caught up with him. But it felt too good to leave this spot and to leave off enjoying his *good buddy, Jack Daniels*. But then Jack Daniels was all gone, Clever staggered out of his truck and checked out the road. He never liked to meet up with any sort of traffic, and there wasn't a lot on Route Ten, but he had to be sure. Clever saw, in his blurred vision, the red SUV coming down the road, and recognized the Coats family vehicle. He leaned on an oak tree watching until the SUV rounded the curve and disappeared out of sight. He gapped up the road and down the road, yelled, "All Clear," and climbed back into his truck. Clever shifted grinding gears, as he backed and banged his way out of the grove of trees and shot across the grassy turf onto the road. Clever Stevens' right foot was heavy on the accelerator while his weighty arms steered into the double and triple burry lanes, of his drunken dark-eyed vision. Clever, the broad, square built, Viet Nam Vet, believed he had done a fine job of maneuvering down such a path, and was proud of his magnificent driving when a big white fuzzy boulder rolled right out in from of him. He bumped it good and sent it flying, but he kept on the purple, blue and pink lanes – all the way home...

6. CHAPTER FIVE

Kate was almost three months old when she left Plum Creek, the brief home she had known with her mother and five brothers, and the humankind that were a part of her infant life on the small Pennsylvania farm. She missed her mother, Shaggy and the little masters most, but she felt secure and comforted with Joe Spangle. The leather jacket that lay next to the metal cage that, held her captive, smelled of the tall humankind man that stole her heart like none other. She felt adrift, yet she knew wherever she might go that she'd be safe with her new Master and Friend. The chewy strip of food Joe Spangle had slipped through the narrow open spaces of the cage was new to Kate, but satisfying, and turning her attention to engaging her small, sharp teeth into bites of the delicious meat was a concentrated effort, and no need for begging for anything more – for the moment.

Even though Kate was completely weaned from Shag, her mother, who stayed with master Levi Coats' large flock of sheep, and she in the Mud Room back at the tall old farmhouse, she still whimpered in her sleep from time to time remembering the innate caring and closeness they'd shared, and the nourishment she'd been given at her mother's pap, and it was at these times she'd felt the gentle caressing of Joe's hands and thought she was still in the big barn with Shag nestled close and warm in her Mother's dense undercoat; but the long drive to Scranton was only the beginning of her journey, and the short time out of the metal cage nestled on Joe's lap was much too brief, but Kate found comfort in the leather jacket that had the scent of her friend and master, Joe Spangle. Her loud puppy protest at loosing site of Shaggy lopping along behind, and at intervals, beside the moving vehicle gave way to the comfort at hand. She gazed out the window, when they came into town, at the city lights, and went wild at the smell of roasted beef at the Arby's Drive through, and was mercifully given a small taste of a different kind of humankind food. She heard Levi and Joe laugh at her barking demand for their lunch, and Levi warning Joe not to make a habit of feeding her *table-food,* and after that she'd fallen asleep until she was lifted out of Levi Coats SUV and put aboard a small aircraft, but with the sound of Joe's crooning voice she'd fallen asleep.

Kate felt the decline of the small Cessna plane as it landed at the Martian- Branson Airway Station for small private planes, as much as she had felt the lifting surge of assent into the sky just outside of Scranton before she'd fallen asleep. She could not see anything, but the soft thro over the doggie tote, and it was all a sense of motion, and she found that she liked the upward thrust as much as the downward glide and barked her pleasure at the landing. Joe Spangle immediately removed the light covering from the metal doggie tote and checked on Kate. "No mess," he said and grinned. He opened the door of the tote and lifted Kate out of the little cage, disembarked his aircraft, and took her off the tarmac to a grassy area for nature's business and to allow her to reclaim her ground legs. Kate was a bit wobbly and she lost her treats, but left it in the grass as she moved to sniff out a particular place for her toiletries.

"Well I can see you might need a little work if you're going to be my Co-Pilot, but what a lady you are Kate-girl, saving your business and upset for the great outdoors! Joe bragged and scooped Kate up and tucked her under his arm feeling his pride in the little pup that pulled on his heartstrings and endeared herself to him in special and particular ways. There was a lot of commotion over Kate in the large Hanger among the men, and in the office at the Martian Airway Station, and Kate endured it all as she tried to hide inside Joe Spangle's leather jacket.   She's a bashful little babe," Greta Martian smiled as she posted Joe's flight information and handed him a computerized copy. "Yes, well she's had quite an experience of 'firsts' Joe said; her first car ride, her first flight, and her first landing."

"I should say she is a brave baby then." Greta replied with a chuckle, and reaching across the counter, patted Kate's bottom that was *open to the breeze.*

"Roger that, but she still has the trip in my jeep out to the farm." Joe said and grimaced at the digging Kate was doing with her puppy claws at his rib cage

"That shouldn't be so bad; at least she will get a look at our great scenic landscape." Greta encouraged sweeping her arms at the view from the station windows, with the green hills in the distance.

"That she will." Joe patted Kate's puppy bottom, which was the only visible part of her from her hiding place beneath his jacket.

"A little rotation might be applied." Greta laughed as she bid Joe Spangle and Kate a nice day. "I think you're right, Greta." Joe agreed looking back at Greta, the pretty, lively daughter of Bill Martian, the owner of the Martian Airway Station- Airport, and an expert pilot of her own Cessna Cub. "Next time you young ladies will meet face to face – I promise." Joe said apologetically, and Greta laughed and waved them goodbye.

The twenty miles drive east to Gentry was a treat to Kate who gazed out of Joe's leather jacket that was zipped up just enough to make a little nest for her hind-end. The late May breeze hit her in the face was cool and exhilarating, while the nest of Joe's jacket was warm. The early evening sun was bright, and Joe slipped on tinted glasses as they left off from smooth paved county roads to dusty and rutted bouncy earthen roads with fenced pasture on either side. Joe talked to Kate at intervals as the jeep bounced along the rutty road to the farm reassuring her that all was well, although Kate seemed to be enjoying the rough ride. The jeep came to a stop in front of a low-slung roofed house with a porch across the front of it. The private road, and circle drive smoothed out with surrounding neat lawns and gardens, Jersey cows and calves were in near pasture with barns small and large, which reminded Kate of her *other place,* although she did not recognize this new kind of *Sheep.* Joe sat in the jeep, pausing to pet his pup, his voice taking on an even and reassuring sound, with a hopeful connotation's in the breath of it. "You and Judith should get along just fine, Kate, he said and scratched playfully at her ears. "You see, she's a little gun-shy of strangers too, so you've got that in common...I'm sure the two of you will be great friends." Joe said with a great sigh and entered the front door of his home with Kate tucked in his jacket, and carrying the doggie tote with bed and packets of food supplies that Janice Coats had sent them away with.

"That you, Mr. Spangle?" Mattie Smyth said teasingly formal with her nephew as she came from the kitchen to greet him. Joe always looked forward to his Aunt's bright smile as much as he did her excellent cooking. He'd rescued his maternal aunt from her disquieting widowhood, and she reveled in taking care of Joe, and later Judith when Joe married.

"Yes, it's I, Mattie. Something smells mighty good even from out here." Joe grinned as she approached him in the foyer.

"I've got supper going, but if you're hungry I can fix you up a bit of an appetizer...Oh and what's this, Joe, you've got in your jacket, for pity sake?" Mattie leaned in, her round gray eyes gazing upon Kate. "Why, what a darlin' fluff of white you got there, Joe Spangle!"

"This is Kate. Kate meet Mattie, the sweetest old lady this side of the great ocean." Joe grinned. "Oh he's a lying to ya about the sweetness, little Kate, but we'll get along, we will."

"She won't be in the house for long, Mattie – she'll get big as a house almost- I'm told, but just for a little while, if you won't mind?" Joe's gray eyes pleaded.

"Why sure, but it's not me you got to convince, Joe, but your sweetheart, and lady of this manor." Mattie said, her eyes twinkling with mirth, for she knew Judith Spangle for her moods, and temperamental bent, and was still terribly fond of the girl.

"And where might my sweetheart be, Mattie?"

"She's gone out for a ride on her pony; I'd say she's been gone for an hour or so, ...should be back any minute, and ready for her salad and tea; and I'll make you a good sandwich, and a cup of good strong coffee…Uh, you want me to take Miss Kate off your hands?"

"No, but thank you Mattie. I'll let Kate loose in the garden so she won't go wandering off quiet yet…I'll be ready for that good coffee after I wash up."

"I might even offer you a piece of my peach pie, Joe Spangle." Mattie teased as she headed back to the kitchen.

"You're a real Peach, Mattie." Joe chuckled as he went out the front door and walked around to the side yard to the clear-"invisible" fenced garden with its wide flagstone terrace where outdoor furniture sat among potted flowering plants and its borders adorned with Dogwood trees. "You'll like it here, Kate, Joe said giving her a treat before setting her down inside the garden gate. It was a different kind of place and one to be explored, and Kate had no inhabitations towards being left to play and snoop in the garden.

Ω

Judith Spangle came in the house from the back porch dressed in Levi's, a blue plaid cotton shirt, and her favorite well broken-in boots. Her dark hair was let down out of her hat, that she perched on a hook by the door. "Darling, you're home!" She exclaimed as her eyes lit up seeing Joe standing near the breakfast bar with a mug of coffee in his hand. Joe sat his mug down and opened his arms. "Gosh I missed you, Joe – you smell funny…" Judith sniffed at Joe's shirt. Joe chuckled and kissed his wife with adore'. "Well I think I smell a little horse on you sweetheart." He teased sniffing loudly.

"Auhh, well that is Ginger's sweet scent, but it's not horsey aroma on you, my love." Judith said as she washed her hands at the sink. "Did you have a good trip Joe? How is the Scranton store doing…any problems?"

"Everything's fine, sweetheart, in fact a bit more profitable than I expected…Joe smiled, as he brought his mug to the table and pulled out a chair for Judith.

"Oh really?" Judith said as she sat down her brows raised at Joe while Mattie served up her salad and tea, and Joe a humongous sandwich, which caused Judith to furl her brow at Mattie. "It's a Manwichsanwich." Mattie said. "And it's a girl he's brought home with him, that's the unexpected profit." Mattie lifted the corners of her mouth in a questionable smile. "But don't worry hon., she's a real dog." Mattie finished, leaving Judith's mouth gaping, as she went for the coffee pot to refill Joe's mug.

"Will someone tell me what's going on here? Mattie is making no sense at all!" Judith exclaimed.   "She does tend to beat around a bush a bit." Joe said and gave Mattie the evil eye. "But she told the truth in her own Irish sort of way. I've brought home a puppy, and she is a girl and a real dog." Joe concluded. "She's a tiny tot at the moment, but she is said to get as big as a house." Mattie explained setting the coffee pot down on the warmer. "Now that it's all out in the open, I leave the two of you to discuss the details. And with a little bow Mattie Smyth departed from the kitchen.

"Don't you just love her?" Joe said wily, and bit into his sandwich.

"Just where is this puppy you've brought home with you? It's one of Levi Coat's Sheepdogs, I assume; and just what do you plan to do with a Sheepdog on a dairy-cow ranch?" Judith questioned insistently.

"Well, Kate, that's her name; Kate can look after most any kind of animals, but mainly I got her 'cause I like her a heck of a lot." Joe said.

"You got a *pet*?" Judith green eyes widen, as Joe Spangle wasn't and never had been the type for pets of any kind.

"Well yes, and no…She's a working dog, but she is loyal to the death for family as well as what herd or flock …whatever kind she might be in charge of." Joe informed as he ducked his head feeling a bit of guilt for not calling and discussing the matter of *Kate* with his wife.

"She sounds wonderful," Judith sighed with little enthusiasm to back up her words. "When can I meet her?" Judith asked. Joe looked up and grinned with relief. He was out of the preverbal doghouse despite Judith's lack of delight. He stood up pulled Judith out of her chair, and kissed her gratefully. "She's out in the garden, and you're going to love her!" He said.

Judith Spangle frowned at the sight of her border flowers uprooted and the sturdy looking puppy rolling around in a pile of compost at the far corner of the garden while Joe only chuckled at Kate's playfulness. She uproots the Verbena, and wallows in the compost!" Judith exclaimed flatly, hands on slender hips.   "Well like Mattie said, sweetheart, the gal I brought home is a *real dog*!" "So I see." Judith said and walked back to the house without further comment. "Uh, she might take a little getting used to…some basic training…" Joe called after his wife as the front door slammed shut.

"Kate!" Joe called. *Katie Love* gave a soft growl in her dreaming, recalling the first scolding she'd gotten from Joe Spangle. She'd instantly stopped her romp in the compost and ran to his feet tail wagging, and licked his dusty boots. Joe ignored her, and on hands and knees he began to bury again what she had dug up. As young as she was, Katie Love recalled knowing that she had done something Joe disapproved of, and that she should not do. She stood aside watching Joe – her head leaning to one side – desiring Joe's *good* attention, but he refused to look at her. She gave a puppy whimper and whine and then turned and helped Joe bury the root-end of the plants she'd up-turned, and this made Joe smile and say, "Good girl, Kate, good girl!" as her back paws slung the soft soil in the general direction of the flowering plants. Katie Love remembered how happy she was to see Joe's smile and hear in his voice the sound of his approval.

7. CHAPTER SIX

"Katie...Katie Love!"

Katie rustled in the hay as she came out of her dreaming and into the present at the sound of Angel's voice. It was her Mistress' modulated voice, a voice that was full of flair and flavor, and one that never made her fearful as voices in her past. She had come almost instantly to love her Mistress, a humankind female that met her with eyes of affection inviting *Kate* with open arms, but waiting for *Kate,* when she was ready, to respond. Ken and 'Angel' Evans, were the couple that renewed her trust in humankind, and delighted her with their two Canines who were just as approving of her as their masters. *Kate,* become "Katie Love," and had been with her present family for six very happy years. She loved the solid, unchanging ties she had with them; they put no harsh conditions on her and seem to understand- at least in part- her desire for unrestrained freedom. Things changed, but not her Master's kindness.

Out of the bright spot of the sun that shined directly on the open side of her Tepee shelter, Katie Love felt the cold winter dampness in every movement of her thighs, shoulders and withers, but it was only lately she'd begun to have such limp and limited movement that not even warmth could undo. She was no longer lissome and agile as she had been when she first came to Ken and Angel, but even then she was not so young; nevertheless, with her new Masters, her *family*, she'd been happier than she had ever been since the days with her own mother, Shaggy. Not only had she two humankind that were unconditionally kind to her, but she had two of her own kind, Jack and Sugar, the black Labradors that welcomed her as lovingly as the human- kind... and what fun they had had together! For Katie Love it was like having a couple of her own siblings in her life. And for the past year or so, there was Annie, *the new kid on the block...* At long last she had a family! Sugar was no longer with them, not since the hot days of August the previous year, which Katie was forgetful of, but Sugar was forever in her heart and memory.

"Come here Katie." Angel stooped and sat a metal bowl of food on the walk, and the old blanket, warmed in the clothes dryer, ready to drape over Katie's old bones she was sure that ached beneath her long shaggy coat. It was useless to invite or entice her indoors out of the often freezing temperatures of wintertime for Katie refused the comforts of confinement. She and Ken had coaxed her into the garage, a few times; the door left up, for Katie would become fearful and upset when it closed. But after a short rest in warmth Katie Love was gone out again into the great outdoors. Only on one below-freezing night was Katie Love compelled to shelter indoors. A great feat of trust her Master's realized, but she ventured only as far as the laundry room that was one door away from the garage, and that was as far as Katie would venture into even comfortable confinement. And only once had Angel been successful in luring Katie Love into the living room, telling her that she should stay indoors with Jack and have her own bed right next to Jack's after some serious grooming, of course. Since Sugar had died, Angle thought it would be a comfort to Jack with Canine Katie Love next to him- and Katie would be protected from, at least, the freezing cold winter days, however; Katie only gave the cozy room a neutral surmising and returned to the garage and then to the great open spaces of the outdoors. There would be no grooming for Katie Love for indoor homing, an impossible fete that Angel never let go of the trying. Meadow and sky, sun and shade were Katie's fortune, and she stubbornly refused to forfeit any of it. Nor would she forge a place where she knew she did not belong.

Katie Love had given little effort at adapting to being enclosed or indoors, and what subtle attempts she had made were only to please her beloved Master and Mistress. However she neither was able to comply with their desire to protect her from inclement weather, nor would she remain–after a great deal of both hardy-heave-ho and gentle persuasion – in a moving vehicle. There were no trips to the Veterinarian or to the Grooming Shop, thus Katie Love's previous and current health status remained a mystery, and her grooming was not part of her winsome ways. Shears and Katie Love just did not mix.

It was a quick turn-about inside the fine, tall wood *den;* Ken had built for Katie Love. She sniffed the new wood, and smelled Ken's familiar scent of soap and sweat, for he had led her into the wide tall doghouse, fit for a canine princess, but left him sitting inside his work of love for a skittish four-pawed *daughter.* Ken wondered if perhaps Katie Love realized immediately that she could not see danger approach tucked inside, and beside that, the wood and hay might limit her sense of smell of anything strange coming upon her Masters home. *How could she protect them cuddled inside such a sturdy dwelling?* No, the outdoors was her tenure, the sky her roof, and the weather her challenge. Katie Love would not fail her loving humankind-family or her Canine brother Jack, and sister, Sugar, who all lived in the confinement of walls and roof, and whom Katie shared looking from the outside in at lighted windows at night; but played and romped with, during the day outdoors, with great delight. And even, with her age- claiming disabilities, Katie Love still had game-playing with her adopted canine brother and sister who were only slightly younger than she – that is until of late... Sugar was gone, and Katie love's strength was diminishing. It was Jack and Sugar that brought her back to activity in her early onset of health decline, and the loving Masters who, in spite of her deep fears, instilled in her a certain spirit of trust.

No, Katie Love had no desire for walls. She was the Protector, the proud Centurion of the night who saved barn kittens and their mother from possums and snakes and helped Jack and Sugar scare away the demolition team of small critters, the Raccoon's, that gnawed wood, and upset the trio of horse's weather they were in pasture or barn. Nothing could deter her from her innate devotion to those she loved and who love her.

"You should come inside, take the winter off from your

determined duties…Oh Katie Love…!" Angel exclaimed softly as she rubbed her tangled hair with the blanket, her brown eyes full of loving and practical concern. Katie ate little, but she brightened at the attention she received from Angel, and licked at the air near Angle's face affectionately. Angel stood, and at Katie Love's failed attempt to stand vertical, on the strength of her stifles, for hugs rent her heart. She bent slightly and hugged Katie's neck. "You know you can come to *Momma* anytime, right?" Katie Love swished her tail and smiled. She understood, *Come to Momma*, and sensed whatever connotation the words that came after might hold, she was confident that they meant something good.

The attention she received from her Mistress, Angel, was health and vigor to her old bones if only temporarily. Katie Love shook of the blanket and was about to take another sTag at a stand-up hug, but sound and scent caught Katie Love's attention and she turned, ears perked at the sight of Little Sammy, the canine friend from down the road, who barked an invitation to roam the pastures. Katie Love felt compelled to oblige, and she knew that exercise was her mainstay hardly secondary to food and water. Angel watched them go, a *Goliath* and *Little King David* canine form, but without the war between them. She sighed, shook her head and hurried back into the house and warmth.

Inside the house, Angel returned to the canvas she'd been working on at the window and   picked-up brush, and palette of small slabs of color; but the bright morning sun had disappeared into the flat gray winter sky. She set aside the palette and gazed out the wide window at Katie Love's large frame in the distance along Elm Tree Road. She could not see Sammy, the small Terrier, because he was, as usual, in the lead. Why Katie Love followed the little critter was simply another mystery of the large winsome Canine that had seemed to have *appeared* into their lives out of nowhere and stolen their heart.   Angel stepped around Jack's elongated bed that lay beneath the window, still feeling the pain of missing Sugar, whose bed had been where she stood now, next to the tripod that held the canvas. She studied the light brush strokes she'd made of Katie Love nestled in the hay beneath the sturdy blue Tepee that Ken had built for her, the sun obscuring sharp lines leaving only the fanciful...That was Katie Love, fanciful, mysterious, and winsome. She'd have to prepare her heart for losing Katie, just as she had for Sugar. The growth of Sugar's tumors had meant a slow and excruciating death, and it was the Vet's recommendation, but her and Ken's decision to have Sugar euthanatized. She had not thought it could be as devastating as when she had to make that decision for her suffering and dying feline, Rocky, six years before, but she was wrong. Sugar had claimed her heart as much as Jack and Rocky, the most companionable cat she'd known– and Katie Love; all three dogs a rescue and each with a story of their own. Angel now had Annie Maria, a young Cocker spaniel mix, a beautiful little canine girl, in great health that had been dumped along the county road and never reclaimed although she'd placed an AD in the local newspaper. Annie's youth and vitality was a blessing to her, although Jack - and dear Sugar, the older dogs, (and Ken who was not into drama), simply ignored Annie's youthful-fantastic antics, bounding around with excessive energy like a *jumping jack* or spinning top– when she chased her tail. It was all a waste of motion as far as Jack and Sugar were concerned. They had no overt reaction, (unlike Ken who fled the room), to Annie's drama only a bored glance and then back to their own agenda, which was lounging, or sniffing about, or sometime listening to their *Momma's* articulate voice carrying on conversations with them or listening to her read aloud. Their energies were spent outdoors with wonderful romps with each other and now with their adopted sister, Katie Love...and Annie trying to keep up with *real dog-play...And with them all, an entourage of Canine's following 'Momma' a mile down the road to the mailbox on warm sunny days...*

    An affection rub with her socked foot where he lay sleeping in his bed, and he grinned and grunted, but was not awakened.

    Angel gave a gray-day sigh and headed for the kitchen. She'd bake Ken's favorite pie, and decorate it with hearts and flowers, mixing her own desired colors from the store-bought food coloring's basic four: Red, Yellow, Blue and Green; her artistry always so much a part of everything about her, and her love of art parallel of her love for canine and feline pets. They were her *children* of four-legs, and her love for them was not measured by performance, but of unconditional love...through sickness and in health... There *was* room for both human and animal on planet earth and in Heaven. She sang as she prepared the pie for her husband, another gift that got her through such cabin-feverish days like this day.

There was something Spanish and American going on in the kitchen which was pleasing to come home to especially on a cold winter's day. Ken was already inhaling the aroma while still in the garage. He was bear hungry and bone chilled, and he wouldn't turn down a hot cup of java- decaf or not, and shouldn't have been surprised when Angle greeted him with a steaming mug, and brown eyes that told him she was glad he was home.

"You read my mind, thanks." He grinned, accepting the mug of coffee and testing a sip then a good gulp. "Everything ok Hon?" Ken asked glancing at the cherry pie cooling on the counter and artfully decorated. Angel usually turned to baking artistry if something was bothering her; unless it was for the Senior Center, or one of her Ladies Clubs.

"You didn't happen to see Katie Love along the road or in the pasture on your way home?" Angel sounded practical, even nonchalant, but Ken knew she was worried about Katie.

"No I didn't, but I wasn't looking for her...could have missed noticing..."

"Katie's kind of hard to miss." Angel half chuckled.

"Well I was just focused on bridging the gaps in the road, I guess." Ken said taking off his coat in the laundry room, and returning to the kitchen and reclaiming his mug of coffee. "How long has she been gone this time?"

"About forty-five minutes. She took off with the Jackson's little ole' dog. How an ounce of a dog like Sammy can lead a hundred and thirty pounds of Katie Love about just by showing up is beyond me!" Angel stirred the Enchilada sauce with a little more vigor than necessary, and Ken chuckled at her ire as he sat down at the Tagle. "For the same reason you are ready to follow Miss Tiny Lady of the Blue Bird Ladies Club whenever she shows up."

"Oh Bennie Berks, you mean? That's entirely different we're working on a project together…uh are you saying I'm poundage?" Angel crooked an eye brow at him as she set the sauce off the burner.

"Noooo, I didn't mean anything like that…" He chuckled again. "Come on, Hon, let's eat I'm as hungry as a polar bear on ice-skates!" Angel smiled. It was always good to have Ken back home…And he would praise her culinary artistry *after* dinner as was his way.

She and Ken spent an enjoyable evening with a couple of games of Rummakube, in which Ken was getting to be worthy competition, and later watching a good movie on the Hallmark channel, a bit of reading before bed…They talked about their mutual concerns for their aging Komondor-Pon Sheepdog; Ken at the end of any hope of getting her inside *anything, anywhere* for the unusually cold winter Missouri was having this year. They had lost Sugar, the big loveable Lab, to cancer in the summer, and now left with Jack and Katie Love, two aging canines - it seemed they were waging a losing battle against death. Ken was more than glad that Angel had the young dog, Annie, to keep them all positive and delighted with her energetic entertainment, though for him, less was more. It seemed no coincident that Annie came into their lives with all of her youthful joy when they needed it most. Not only had they lost their beloved pets, including Bunny, Ken's pet calf left motherless, but Angel's dear mother, whom she'd nursed, loved and cared for the latter years of her long life. Barbara-"Angel" Evans was a strong vibrant woman and a loving wife. She is "Angel" to Ken, to Katie Love, dear old Jack and Sugar, and to frisky Annie, all rescued by 'Angel's' Love; the still lovely olive-skinned, brown-eyed beauty that Kenneth Evans married twenty-five years ago and called her, "My Angel."

8. CHAPTER SEVEN

The following morning Ken Evans stood at the expansive dining room window that provided a panorama view of the front yard and circle drive. In the center of the yard was the square of tile with twin planters of sleeping Knock-Out Roses awaiting spring. To his right was the empty trailer home they had bought for his mother in-law and that now served as a guest house for visiting family that were between career choices or in need of the country quiet . A short distance away stood the huge royal-blue and silver barn, a polygonal roof its crown; and inside; its mix of tools, a worktable, a lame vehicle, farm machinery, and odds and ends of old furniture here and there; and the sacks of feed & hay on thick wooden pallets. The worktable was one of Ken's favorite places where he gathered a good deal of satisfaction repairing car and machinery parts; and broken chairs and kitchen gadgets for Angel. It was also the indoor place with it's wide open door that he had many conversations with Katie, but she'd later refused to shelter in the barn, because the door needed closed at night against rain and cold to protect expensive farm equipment, and possible collection of small and large animals looking for shelter; and against human thieves who prowled the night. Katie would have deterred the thieves, but she might have been shot and killed in the process. Katie Love was always for taking risk out in the open under the heat of the sun in summer, and the moon chill of winter nights. She was a sweet, brave, and mysterious creature, that not even *Momma* with her own unique talent with canines could quiet figure out, and tame, for the full extent of the loving care she longed to give the big loving, endearing creature that was Katie Love. To the left of the barn nearer the house stood the large sturdy Tepee with its triple, bright-blue plastic and vinyl topping he'd put together for Katie; one side open to the elements, a needed concession to accommodate Katie's sever phobia of enclosed spaces. He had only a partial peripheral view of the handsome house, that stood near the house beneath the living-room window, he had built for Katie Love; and only after days of patient persuasions she'd reluctantly followed him inside, which resulted in a momentary house inspection, before she U-turned out and left him sitting there head drooped in defeat. Katie never set paw near the beautiful dog house again. Jack had put the big canine house to use, for sheltered rest, in order to extend his outdoor time of play and adventure along with Katie Love, and Sugar before her demise, and for practical purposes if Mistress & Master were delayed returning home from business or outings.

But now Sugar was dead and Katie Love ailing and partially lame; and the kid, Annie, a nuances of energy; an insulting reminder of their vibrant younger years; and Ken's ailing knees giving him the same aggravation. Even so, Jack could still give Annie a run; for the sake of his pride, and Katie Love would give Annie Marie a go at it too- on a good sun-filled day, nor would Ken be defeated by painful knee joints.

Ken watched the mound of hay, where Katie had tunneled into for the night, her twitching tail revealing her hide-a-bed. Ken chuckled at the sight of the moving hay as if a rodent or Raccoon were lost in the hay stack and blindly searching a way out.

"Well good morning Love," Angel croaked still sleep laden. "You shouldn't look so happy this early it's intimidating."

"I made coffee. Grab a cup and come take a look at what humors me." Ken grinned.

"I'll be right with you." Angel smiled in spite of her ragged night. She'd tightened the ties of her robe, poured a cup of fresh coffee and stepped across the kitchen to the dining area and stood next to Ken.

"Rough night?" Ken asked and draped an arm across her shoulder. He had slept soundly upstairs in the spacious loft, a concession he and Angel had agreed to because of his radical snoring sleep.

"Katie didn't come home 'til after midnight…I happened to

have been up...and no, I didn't wait up." Angel quickly informed at Ken's inquiring look. Ken squeezed her close, and nodded toward the window and the outdoors. Angel craned forward following Ken's focus. He nodded toward the left. "Look." He said, snickering over the moving mound of hay. Jack, the big lab, moseyed into the dining room, paused and stared a moment at his Mistress and Master. With a leisurely gait across the floor Jack pried a space between them, and stood on his haunches his large paws pressed against the window sill. Ken gave way to Jack, but Jack sided up close to Angel. "Ok, Momma's Boy have it your way." Ken said.   Jack barked his reply, and ken and Angel laughed at Jack's obvious favoritism. Labrador Jack leaned his head to the left taking in the entertainment with Momma and Ken. And indeed Angel was Momma to Jack since the days of his vicarious puppy-hood:

The hard-nailed old farmer was railing against the family's Bitch-hunter's litter of pups with a shotgun full of spreading lead. Time was up for his wife to have found homes for the puppies and Farmer Orville "Oddie" Drake wasn't raise'n a bunch of illegitimate half-breeds! Angel got a frantic call from her daughter, Angelina, the mailperson on the country route where the gun-slinging old farmer lived. "There's one left, hiding under the house...Hurry Mom!" Angel hit the road in the Jeep, and bit the speed limit and prayed, as she had a mental picture of a yard full of murdered puppies. She needn't have worried of finding the right house for the heartless old farmer was standing on his wide front porch with shotgun in hand, while neighbors were running into the woods to find the terrified puppies. "Don't shoot! Don't shoot!" Angel yelled as she stooped on all fours to find the pup beneath the porch. "I'll take this one off your hands!" She said, and spent some time urging the shaking little Labrador puppy into the safety of her arms. The wife of the contrary old farmer appeared timidly on the porch after the shotgun blasts ceased when Angel arrival on the scene. "That's no way to find decent homes for the pups, Orville!" She said. "Folks came didn't they?" Orville retorted hatefully. Several women, and a couple of big boys came out of the woods carrying puppies cradled in their arms. One brave lady from a neighboring farm came up to the porch and looked up at the old farmer. "I think we got 'em all Oddie." She said and hurried off. Angel stared at the mean, angry old man with unbelieving eyes as she nestled the terrified puppy in her arms. The old farmer stared back into Angle's own angry eyes. "Good thing, 'cause I'd of killed the all of em!" He snarled and slammed into the house directing his wife to follow with a quick motion of his hand. Later on it was proven that Jack was no half-breed, and Angel wondered if the cranky old farmer ever realized what he'd scared- to- death- away.

Angel pulled Jack against her hip and nestled his dear face. "Come along Jackie Boy, I'll let you out to go pee." Jack was always happy to be let out doors, but he was accustom to his warm and comfort indoors with his Mistress and Master, and had no problem with all such amenities: Cool in the heat of summer and warmth in the cold of wintertime. "Jack, Katie is sleeping."Angel said. "Be very quiet," she said lowering her voice to a whisper. Jack complied, his anticipation giving way to a lazy straggle across the yard towards his favorite tree.

Ken and Angel watched from the window as Jack crept silently back across the yard and stood at the open side of Katie Love's digs. He watched the hay move, ready to pounce, but stole a glance at *Momma*, in the wide window, to see if she was still watching and for a sign of approval; but Angel shook her head in the negative. In compliance, Jack gave a stoop shoulder- drop of his ready stance when suddenly Katie Love leapt from the hay barking a good morning to her *adopted* brother causing him to jump backward in shocked surprise. Their canine grin's were pronounced and obvious as they both bounded off after Jack's quick recovery, and Katie *wee'd* where Jack had just pee'd.

Inside the house Angel and Ken were breaking up with laughter, for Jack had jump two feet at the unexpected leap Katie took out of the hay. "How could she have managed such a leap, when she could hardly walk yesterday afternoon?" Angel demanded in amazement.

"Maybe it's a bit like my knees, Ken replied. "I have my good days and I have my *really* bad days." He shrugged at what simplicity he made of difficult things.

"How are your knees today?" Angel inquired seriously as she stepped into the kitchen to prepare breakfast. "So far so good." Ken said as he joined her and prepared to butter bread for the toaster oven.

Annie came hurrying into the kitchen at the awakening smell of bacon, which she would not get, and Angel paused to welcome her "baby" to the day and let her out. Annie had earned a place of respect with the older siblings, and they welcomed the pretty little sister to their circle of play.

"Katie seems in a good receptive mood, feeling so well; should we try to get her in the SUV and take her to the Vet and for grooming?" Angel asked as they lingered over breakfast.

"You know that's a lost cause, Angel." Ken said lifting his brow at his wife. "If she bailed out of the open bed of the pickup – again and again - she's not going to tolerate the enclosure of the SUV…"

"Yeah, I know. Angel sighed. It's just that she seems so well and happy…I guess seeing her this way gave me new hope."

"We'll have to take one day at a time doing our best for the three of them, for Katie Love…It's all… we can do… we're all in God's hands." Ken said with his practical and faithful way.

"You are right Babe" Angel smiled. We will enjoy every minute of this day…and look how bright the sun today!" Angel exclaimed nodding at the beaming sun against the windowpane.

"It is ten degrees warmer than yesterday all ready." Ken remarked. I checked the outdoor thermometer earlier when I was out feeding the horses and letting them out to pasture."

"That farmer son's clock is still ticking loudly…Angel commented lightly. How is Dixie and Prince…doing, okay?" They had found a good home for "Red," but Prince and Dixie were not trained for riding horses, and that's what prospective buyer were looking for. Nature was having her way with the down-sizing of canine and feline pets: the sweet barn cat and her kittens by way of Tick Fever. Cancerous, obtrusive tumors had claimed Sugar, and another type of Cancer took Rocky the silky Siamese cat. Bunny, the little calf, died for lack of her Mother's milk, and age was rapidly taking hold of dear, sweet Jack, and Katie Love…but with Katie her own fears and obstinacy leaned heavily toward her demise…So Ken was even more determined to take good care of Dixie and Prince, the two quarter horses he'd raised from colts… unless trusted family members decided to pasture and care for them…when his knees would prevent his doing so.

"Better today for the good sunshine – like the rest of us." Ken said of his horses and his knees. "I think I better take you out on the town or out of town today while we have the chance." Ken smiled. And Angel shook her head in the affirmative with enthusiasm. It was agreed that they would not talk about the animals. This was *their* day together, a day for enjoying the break in the weather, for that was all it was according to the TV Weather Station's report. The near freezing and possible freezing weather would return. As it happened, they each took a guilty breath a few times whenever they almost broke the bargain, and laughed at both their obsession with beloved pets. But they managed to keep *the kids on the back burner while they* enjoyed shopping out of town, and lunching at a unique little café in Bow Hollow, and a welcomed impromptu visit with dear friends along the way. They stayed out as long as they could, their last stop at the *Antique Shop*, both happy with their 'finds' and purchases; Ken his special tool, and Angel an *artistic* lamp, that Ken was sure would end up in the barn…

9. CHAPTER EIGHT

There were many better and happier days with their rescued and adopted canine family when they were younger; and the pets were younger and in prime health. The protection the Lab's and Katie Love provided for them and their home out in the "Boonies," as one of their City Friend's called it, was only part of the benefit of their company. It was not always true that 'Man's Best Friend" was canine; however it was very close to an absolute. They would work and strive right beside you, and risk their lives to save you from harm. Their unconditional love was an unexplainable joy, and what little they asked in return was minimal and doable for the most of them…Katie Love seemed to be the only exception to that rule in Angel's long experience with her beloved Lab's.

Of course Katie was a mature female dog when she saw Ken Evans across the lane in his pasture land just below the knoll. The pasture generously sprinkled with wild flowers, of bluish-purple, and clusters of the bright yellow petals of the meadow-daisy, was Kate-Katie's playground. She barked her greeting and stood with shifting paws unsure of what kind of human the slender-built, silver-haired man might be. He came toward her with a smile on his face, and a low encouraging whistle, but Katie-Love, who was vaguely "Kate" at this time, bounded away as if she had wings when the kind-appearing human got too close. It took time to build what was a very vicarious relationship with the big, beautiful, shaggy sheepdog, but after a couple of weeks of open invitation: of smiles, fresh food and water, and large cookie treats, Kate was convinced this humankind could be trusted. She came, trotting across pasture, and sat down with Ken on the level place just below the knoll. Ken talked and *Kate* listened, her smile, and the movement of her ears and the occasional swish of her tail was evidence that she was enjoying the communing; and Ken was confident that she understood more than he was apt to give her credit for. When Angel, curious, asked, "What do you talk to Katie about out there in the barn?" Ken only chuckled and said, teasingly, "I don't talk and tell."

Kate gave Angel a wide berth for a week, but with the Lady human, who instantly called her Katie-Love it was only a matter of being assured it was *ok* with Master Ken for her to share her affection with *Angel*. The next step was to watch Angel, and the two large ones like herself, except they were dark and of a shiny slick coat, while she was even larger with a mount of matted and tangled white hair. The big black Lab's, one with white markings, and the other one with the brown markings, Katie recognized as female. She was called "Sugar, and the larger one, the male-factor, was called Jack. Katie enjoyed watching the interaction of the humankind with the ones like herself. It had been long ago that she'd seen or experienced the like of it...The three invited and waited. There was no rush...for they were enjoying the game of chasing the ball that was tossed from the hand of their Mistress... which gave Kate – Katie Love flashes of long-ago memories.

Katie Love sensed that her new Mistress was not at all like her Mistress of the past, *Judith Spangle.* Katie did not like to think of the past, that latter part of her youth spent locked up in a metal cage not big enough to turn around in. These memories made her fidgety. She felt a fierce rage when she remembered such things and the only way to free herself from such fearful things was to run loose and free. But with Angel's firm kindness those memories faded. Her voice was not full of vicious demeaning accusations- and threats with a large pair of hedge clippers- like her other Mistress; but a good kind of talk and wonderful play! The canine siblings were as full of fun and favor as the kind Mistress. And the gentle Master with whom she shared that particular communication, was with his soothing talk, a constant reminder of her childhood Master, Joe Spangle. They were unalike in their physical image, but Ken was the personification of the humankind Master of her puppyhood to her coming of age...

the per foliation of two so different and yet so much alike, and Mistress Angel was as kind as Katie's, *friend,* Ken.

At present Katie Love and her pal, Jack, were returning from a long outing in the pasture and woods. The day was much warmer, than previous days, and Katie's bone-joints seemed renewed. She was especially happy to have had her *brother* along for the trek in the pasture and woods; but little Annie Marie, gone-off with the Master & Mistress, was left with a friend in town. It was something Jack or Sugar, in their early days together with Katie Love would never do if Angel-M*omma* was at home. They never left the perimeter of the yard all around the house without *Momma's* consent. Katie had learned from Jack and Sugar what *Guard The Yard* meant, and at the command the three of them gave a loud, vicious growling- bark to warn away any intruder, human or animal, friend or foe…It was true that she had influenced Jack and Sugar's natural instinct to join her in that social and secure *pack* of adventure away from the humankind, but Katie Love was sure to bring them home again in-tact and unharmed before their dear Mistress and Master returned home. And Katie Love *knew* that the Lab's would have no difficulty navigating their way home, on their own. It was also apparent to Komondor Katie that Jack and Sugar would never leave their humankind and home even for a life with *The Pack.* And Katie was beginning to have that same kind of connection.

In those early days with her new family, Katie joined her canine siblings and Mistress Angel in games of ball after she'd stood aside and watched their play for a few days. She only caught the tennis ball in her mouth, jumping high to catch it in the air, and pouncing low, to stop the rolling ball with her big paw and carrying it in her mouth to Angel's feet. It was Jack and Sugar who on a turn of a dime darted after the long throw's away that Angel tossed in various tricks to put them off direction, but they both knew where to sniff out the ball even if they did not see the direction of the toss. They loved the *seek & find* while Katie loved the *catch & bring.* Katie stood aside and watched, never interfering with the *retrieving* of the ball. She liked to watch, but it was not her game, and she soon left the scene for a tramp in the woods.

Katie Love was very sorry she'd left home on one particular spring day. She hadn't meant to scare the small creature with the fluffy tail, and a white stripe down its otherwise black body. It was a shock to her system when the cute little critter made a sudden stop lifted her tail and sprayed her with a breath choking scent. She'd gone home, half blind, needing help and desiring comfort, but Jack and Sugar ran her off - and *guarded the yard* So Katie sat at the end of the driveway and waited for Mistress Angel to return home from her Club meeting, and help her out of her mess of trouble. The car drew up and Katie put on her most forlorn face, and it took little effort for her misery was all too real. Angel lowered the window only to fly it up again, her smile recoiling into pinched disgust. She drove on down the long drive and parked in the garage. Jack and Sugar barked at any attempts Katie made to follow Angel's car near the house and *them*. Katie sat sad-faced and watched as Mistress Angel let Jack and Sugar inside the house, their barking exchanged for box seats at the living-room window. The garage door came up and Angel came out lugging a huge tub with a plastic bottle of Dawn, a jar of mustard and a water hose. Ken came home from the hill, where he'd been feeding the cows, with a red bandanna over his nose and mouth as he approached the yard.

The tub was being filled with water and blue liquid that made white clouds of suds. This was not the kind of help Katie had in mind…Ken took over the water hose, the red thing still held over his nose, while Angel, a scarf tied bandit style over her face, offered up big round cookies, the very thing Katie could not resist, and in her state, she needed something to take her mind off her stinging red eyes , and sneezing, runny nose, and the smell… she didn't mind a roll in nature's compost, but this was something no dog should have to endure! Katie came after the big cookies in a smelly trot, but Angel held them high, and said "Wait!" She pointed to the tub, and Katie bulked, she caught sight of Jack and Sugar now holding front-row tickets in the dining room window.

They barked when she made eye contact, letting her know they were not coming near her...unless...Their heads bobbed at the tub. *Get in or get out!* seemed to be their given choices to her. Katie got in the tub. She got her cookies from one stage to the next of her de-skunking bath...Angel tossed the last cookie on the grass and she and Ken ran for cover in the garage to avoid Katie's great shake and spin dry of her long very wet hair. It had never been so easy to get Katie Love in a bath on the rare occasions that she didn't head for the hills. Ken and Angel were very wet and very proud.

After that, somewhat taming experience, Katie Love began to stay close to her new home. Rarely did she leave the yard unless it was a trek to the pasture with Ken. The cows, she chose to "hang with" before Ken, she happily attended with him.

Katie's presence in the yard kept the rabbits, raccoons, opossums, and the little foxes at bay, but the squirrels, though cautious and quick on the ground, were keeping house in the oak and elm trees in the yard. Katie was also a determent to the larger animal kingdom around the woods near the house, wolves, deer and the occasional snorting pig that escaped a pen somewhere. These were the rarer or occasional visitors and the lone wolf the most frightening. If Angel heard the howl of a wolf nearby, she let the Lab's out to *Guard The Yard* with Katie, the Komondor, and the sight of three large canines baring their fangs in the moonlight was sufficient for even the Wolf to high-tail it back from where he came. Even so, Angel was breathless until it was all over; fearing for the lives of her Labs and Katie Love if a brazen wild wolf came over the fenced wooded pasture. The Lab's would take it on – first, because they were much more swift and agile than Katie-Love, these days. But Angel believed that Katie Love had long experience in fighting, and that her poundage would give her the greater advantage, therefore Angel prayed the Lab's would keep her command of Guarding the Yard...staying within the boundaries of their own territory, and that any wolf would be scared away by the real threat of her beloved Canines. As Katie Love lingered at home more and more the Mistress and Master Evans were the more inspired to get her to a Veterinarian for a health checkup, and to the local Dog Groomer. This was summer months of devising ways and means of getting the 130 pound Komondor into the back of the pickup for transport. They soon concluded after many failed attempts of luring with food, pushing and pulling, and giving her rump a heave-ho, that Katie Love was *most* receptive to the pickup-bed as long as Ken was in there with her. Uh –ha! Angel would do the driving, and Ken, the soothing Shaggy-Dog Whisperer, would be Katie's *keeper in the truck-bed*. Perfect! Until the pick-up truck begin to move, and Katie went ballistic leaping over the tailgate, and then to hide her refusal to comply, she made a playful game on the ground of "Catch Me" She was as agile, and as quick as mountain goat, back then, and as ornery, when it came to any sort of confinement or transport. And in the end when she had worn out two fine senior citizens she was all sweetness and apology. Katie Love was hard to resist for all her freedom fighting ways…

Angel had succeeded in loving Katie into an occasional very quick trim with a *small* pair of scissors, and the rare water-hose baths. The longest Katie Love had ever stood still for any sort of grooming was when she came from the pastures with a piece of barbwire entangled in her long shaggy hair. It was a work of patience's and careful analysis for any prick or pain at the hands of humankind would send Katie Love over the edge and into the woods…possibly never to return…Katie Love was low maintenance, but high calibrate when it came to understanding her *needs*.

The last effort to bring Katie Love to the Vet was the Veterinarian doctor's own suggestion of dosing her with three Benadryl Tabs mixed in her food. She would become sleepily relaxed and easy to leash and led into the back of the truck where she'd fall asleep with Ken's soothing commune…and on to the Vets – Walla! Not so with Katie Love and her intelligent sense of self-preservation. She became anxious as soon as she felt the effects of the Benadryl, and her innate reaction was to get up and *move*! Katie staggered and put *herself* in the tightest of places at the low end of the Trailer Home's slanting ramp off its fenced porch. It was Angel's very independent Mother's home until her health determined she move into the house with her daughter and son in-law until the good Lord took her *home.* Katie locked herself in that tiny place for protection, a place she normally would avoid at all cost, and slept-off the effects of the relaxer, and left a sorry and regretful Mistress and Master to worry. That was the end of any further thoughts of getting Katie Love to the Vet or groomed. They would accept her "as is" and leave the consequence to God and Nature. Katie Love woke from her sound sleep later in the evening and was the same loving, perking and playful 'Katie' as she'd always been. No harm done. Angel and Ken wept with relief.

From that time on Katie Love would run at the first whip of normal dog-caring medicine. For some unexplainable reason she liked the Tick medicine, and what self-respecting Tick, they wondered, would attempt to find its way beneath all Katie's thick shaggy coat to her skin? It seemed to Ken it would die from starvation before it ever got near its food source. It was much less work for Angel and Ken to just let Katie be Katie. Whatever her phobias, and fears, they hadn't the power to fix, and what they could offer was plenty of love, and healthy food.

And that's how it was- their years with Katie Love, until the last year and the hard winter. She had begun to slow down, her playtime minimal, her sleep maximized. As Katie had from the start of their relationship, she still refused the comfort of any kind of confinement. She had begun to wonder off and stay gone hours, but so far, she always returned home.

The country community was growing and changing. Two new families had bought land and built homes near the Evans land, and others were building in the Elm Tree community.

Ken and Angel loved their pretty gray and white country home with its wide inviting porch across the front, and the interior furnished with an Artist's style and warmth. They both enjoyed the privacy and the freedom they had with their beloved pets, and simply the beauty, fresh air and quietness of the countryside. However, they appreciated good neighbors, and welcomed those nearby with open heart. After ten years on Elm

Tree Road, they now had a brand new mailbox within steps from the house. And still a trio to escort Angel to pick-up the mail: Jack, Katie, and Annie Marie…Soon it would only be the baby, Annie…

10. CHAPTER NINE

Katie Love had been making frequent treks out and about with Little Sammy, the Jackson's small Terrier, since that bright sunny day over a week ago. The *Odd Couple* was sometimes joined by the mixer, Digger, who promptly left their pack when Little Sammy, with his insistent yapping, was determined to lead them further into the woods to some particular place he repeatedly brought them to. Sammy was not concerned with Digger leaving them, for it was Katie Love he wanted to show his treasure. So far Katie had refused to go the distance, and Little Sammy sensed that Katie's strength was diminishing a little each day, and it seemed all the more urgent that she follow him to that purlieu just beyond the woods. So far they came to within two miles of the place, and that seemed to be the point where Digger refused to go beyond as if the more prominent breed of Redbone Hound in him could smell danger that he or Katie were able to determine. Sammy hurried on ahead his short, skinny legs moving in quick, rapid steps, but he'd only gotten a hundred yards away from where Katie stood, before she barked a harsh warning for him to return. The winter's chill was dropping with the lowering of the sun, and the young robust little Terrier was aware of the danger, and other dangers of the woods, that he might not be able to out-run when the odds were stacked against him. He was quiet safe with just the presence of Katie, but with her limited strength Sammy wondered if she could prevail if she had to defend herself and him? He stopped and turned and ran as fast has his little legs would carry him back to Katie Love.

Back on Elm Tree Road, the few and far-between houses were pleasant sights with their lighted windows and aromatic smoke that drifted from chimneys, warming the evening air. The door at the Jackson's house flew open at the first sound of Little Sammy's high-pitched yapping. "Where the hell-bells have you been, you little squirt?" The bald-headed man said picking up Sammy, and Sammy licking-face to avoid any possible consequence. The man looked out on the road and noticed Katie paused in the spot of yellow porch light. "Thanks for bringing Sammy home safe, Katie Love," he said. "Now you go on home and get warm 'old girl." Katie grinned and waved her tail, and jogged a yard until she heard the door close, and slowed to a walk the rest of the way home. Doors were opened to Katie Love too; Angel at the front door with a welcome, and Ken raising the garage door and beckoning Katie inside, but she smiled and swished a wave of her tail at her beloved Mistress & Momma, Angel, and Master & Friend, Ken, but turned to her Teepee and settled in for a nap. Angel sent Ken out with an old water repellent camping comforter, and after a short talk Katie Love accepted the large quilt laid over her. Her coat was dry, for the day had been very brisk and cold, but the air dry; a needed change. It was only her big paws and hocks that were damp and dirty, and the hay would help both those conditions. Jack had been there at the door with "Momma" his welcoming grin, and his tail wagging his delight at seeing Katie Love. She gave a bark of greeting especially for Jack, and he answered her and returned to his bed, satisfied that his *sister* was home from the woods.

  Katie Love had nothing on her mind but warmth and rest, but her hunger and thirst woke her from her early evening nap, and she moseyed to the front porch where her water and metal food bowl set with meaty tasting, chewy and crunchy chunks of food, and the water exhilaratingly cold and refreshing. Katie hadn't taken to the battery operated water warmer, Angel had gotten for her to keep her water from freezing. The water was Luke-warm, and the buzz and vibration that came from the battery-powered bowl seemed like something *alive* and *unsafe*. Katie didn't mind melting ice cubes in her water in the summer, for they were silent and cool, but tepid water had never been her favorite, especially tepid water that 'talked.' Her refusal to drink from it brought back the earthenware bowl that had no suspicious sounds and the cold water that she preferred. Katie, after she'd taken nourishment, gave a long and elaborate security check around the house, she gazed her night-vision eyes on a baby garden snake, and watched it slither under the barbwire fence that squared-off to the west and into the woods. If she heard the howl of a wolf, or smelled one too nearby she stood her watch along the fence line, baring her fangs, and snarling out her warning, lifting her shoulders and pushing out her brisket filling her lungs with air. She trotted along the yard-side of the fence at her best fighting stature, her head and tail down, but her big head moving to keep alert of movement and odor of any threat. She saw and heard and smelled only little creatures, the small animals that might have been *her* prey if she were out in the woods for a length of time. After several hours on the job, Katie gave-in to the quiet of the night and settled in for dosing sleep.

 Katie tunneled into the hay, beneath the big camper comforter her eyes, nose and ears on alert even while she slept. She sunk into a dreamless sleep, but only for a short time before she began to dream of her young years with friend, and master, Joe Spangle. She was called "Kate" back then, but never Katie, which had more of an extended sound to it, and an lyrical upsweep that caught her likening right away. Perhaps it was the voice that named her...Angel's voice that made her so content with her name, Katie Love. She dreamed...

 As a pup- and Joe's "Kate," she was often in the clouds way up in the sky within a big metal bird with wings that didn't move, except the noisy propeller one attached to its nose. Kate was set in a *car seat* next to Joe, when she was small, and taken to different but similar places, where she met a lot of smiling humankind. She liked the smell of shoe leather, and clothing made of lamb's wool, combed cotton, and brushed leather that her senses experienced in the Spangle Sports Shop's that she visited with Joe; and the fuss the humankind made over her at every visit. It was a difficult adjustment to stay grounded when she grew too large for the small Cessna plane, while Joe drove his jeep to the airport to fly away in the blue and silver metal bird alone. She had reached her full size and Maturity in her fourth year with Joe Spangle. She was healthy and spaded, and a happy canine, except when she was in the presence of Judith Spangle. Kate had given her best to be a friend to Judith, but without success. She longed to be with her friend and master, Joe, but she had outgrown his metal bird. Joe had introduced her to his dairy cows early on, and when she was not flying around the country with Joe, she was with the little calves, and when they were put in a separate pasture to wean them away from their mother, Kate pastured with them comforting them from crying after their mother, and protecting them from the danger of other animals and from poachers. There had been occasions when Kate had to leap over the fence to protect the breeder cows from blatant rustlers. The sight of her flying over the fence, fangs bared was enough to scare off the rustlers, until they returned with guns. Kate was glazed by a bullet twice, but she was to agile and fast for the crooks to get a good shot at her, and when she had mangled one culprit's hand and arm so badly -wrestling the weapon from him, the gang never returned. There was the humankind security that rode about the house and pasture in a big dually truck at intervals, but what they missed in-between their tours of duty and off duty, Kate took care of quiet well. The security men and Judith had some unwarranted fear of Kate, and even though she was praised by the men they never wanted anything to do with Kate.

  Judith's fear sprang from Jealousy. The Mistress of the Spangle home hated anyone or anything that *her* Joe treasured – such as his Sports Shops. And it was all too obvious that Joe Spangle treasured his dog, Kate. Mattie Smyth, Joe's Aunt, was a measure of protection against Judith Spangle's dual personality – for at times she could be ever so kind, but her kindness could flip over to hatefulness and meanness in a matter of dark invading minutes. While Mattie always took the direct approach with Judith, she was never mean. Mattie spoke her mind in a straight forward manner, and never backed down to Judith Spangle's temperamental attitudes and hatefulness, for which Judith seemed to hold some respect. Kate simply left when Judith came near, but not without a string of name-calling following after her; and threats, which were easily understood by the sound of Judith's voice, the look of her green eyes, and the handgun, or some garden tool she raised at Kate. Eventually Kate stayed in the pasture with the cows and calves, and never came near the Spangle's home until Joe returned from his flights and gave his familiar whistle. Kate would run to Flax Robinson or one of his three young son's Tad, Billy, and Toby, for her *official* leave taking. "Boss is calling" they'd say and give a nod of consent and Kate would break-fence and run to met Joe Spangle with her big canine grin.

Infrequently Joe would take Kate to the Jenkins Farm down the road and to Mrs. Jenkins for bath and grooming. This had been done since Kate was a pup, and although Kate was not enthused about it she knew it pleased Joe, therefore she endured the process; and came to a very good relationship with Mrs. Jenkins, who talked to her all through the process, and gave Kate treats, rewarding her woebegone cooperation. Kate always approached this particular necessity with head down and tail between her legs, but afterwards, she was a happy camper, which made the Jenkins's and Joe laugh at Kate's same rendering attitude at each grooming.

Mattie Smyth was another love of Kate's and a constant arbitrator between Kate and Judith Spangle, although when Joe was home Judith was sugary-sweet towards Kate, which did not fool Kate or Mattie. Judith had made an attempt to run-over Kate while she was out riding on her horse, Ginger, however the beautiful brown and white Mare bucked and snorted in protest, almost throwing Judith off her back. In retaliation the furious rider whipped at her own beloved animal mercilessly, and spent three days chasing Kate who took the woods, but Kate always returned to the little calves in pasture when Judith had given up the pursuit. Judith rode the rogue Stallion for her search after Kate, for she could not trust Ginger for such a deed of intending harm, but Kate was quick to remove herself from harm's way when she caught the scent of Judith and her steed.

Judith had managed to bribe one of the Security Guards,

Rick Mason, to catch Kate, and put her in the small metal cage and hide her back in the woods in an old shackled, one-room log cabin. When Mason protested at the tight cage Judith had brought to house the drugged and sleeping Kate, she only reminded him that his thousand dollar pay for the job depended on his following her orders. The muscled young man, who had a high-maintenance girlfriend, and a sensual respect for Judith's horsemanship and *brass*, took the cash that Judith waved in his handsome face, and with great effort, lifted the dead- weight of Kate into the cage. Kate would have no room to stand, except in a very slumped position, and there was no room for movement... She was captured and jailed, the padlock on the cage door was unbreakable.

Mattie Smyth, sister to Joe Spangle's mother, (and Joe's highly paid Cook and Housekeeper, since her widowhood), worried when Kate went missing for three days. The Robinson's boys insisted it was not like Kate to leave the calves she loved to tend, so they were concerned and puzzled. Mattie began to look at Judith with suspicion and dread. Flax Robison, Joe's friend and right-hand man on the farm, gave his boys leave to go look for Kate on their four wheelers, taking their own russet Lab, Bell, to help in the search. They gave Bell a sniff of Kate's bed on the back porch of the house, Judith Spangle looking on angrily from the window. She let the kitchen curtain drop her breath heavy with wrath as she stormed past Mattie who busied herself testing the state of her homemade yeast bread and its rising. As soon as Mattie heard Judith's stormy footsteps on the stairs and the slamming of her bedroom door she hurried to the porch. "You boys be careful out there, and if you find Kate...sick, injured or dead...God forbid...well you leave her be, and I'll get Mr. Jenkins and his crew to bring her home..."

"Auh' Kate's alright, Miz' Smyth, Toby said. She's just out wondering the woods, taking a little vacation...you might say..." Billy and Tad averted their eyes at the falsehood, but they knew their big brother, Toby, was only trying to comfort a worrying lady. "Come on, Toby, we'd better get started while there's daylight." Billy said, and the boys gave a nod of respect to Mattie and set off on their four wheelers, with Bell keeping up, ready for the search.

Mattie Smyth called Koki Spangle, Joe's mother, and her baby sister. "Koki have you heard from Joe?" From her condo on the beaches of Florida, Koki, a younger, more sophisticated version of Mattie replied: "Mattie dear, Joe has no cell service where he's at up North. He can't contact anyone unless they come down off the river and into town...Oh he's enjoying river-rafting with Levi and a couple of his old Military buddies, he did tell me that before they got off so far..." Is anything wrong, Mattie...Judith...is she *alright?*"

"It's Kate, Joe's dog. She's been missing for three days now...and well you have no idea what that big sweet dog means to Joe!" Mattie exclaimed.

"Well, I have a pretty good idea dear, but dogs do go off on the roam sometimes..."

"Not Kate. She never does, unless she with Joe trekking the woods." Mattie explained.

"Well let's not worry Joe with the matter just yet...he seldom gets together with his friends...let's not spoil his vacation, Sis." Koki insisted.

"Well, we have the Robinson boys, and their Lab, out searching the woods for Kate...Koki I think Judith had something to do with Kate's disappearance – that's what worries me...she hates that poor dog and for no reason!"

"She's a troubled girl, that wife of Joe's!" Koki exclaimed. "I'll have Joe call you if I should hear from him. In the meantime, Mattie, don't upset yourself. I love you dear, take care. Bye, Love... The connection was broken and Mattie felt no better.

11. CHAPTER TEN

"Why did you do it, Judith?"

Joe's question was spoken soft and full of sorrow. That big shaggy dog would never hurt you, in fact she'd give her life to protect you!" Joe exclaimed quietly.

"Are you so sure?" Judith looked up from her packing, her green eyes sharp and angry. "That dog you care so much about almost caused my horse to throw me trying to avoid stomping over the stupid creature!" Judith knew it was a lie, but she had to twist things around in her mind to suit her own purposes.

"That's not what happened and you know it, Judith. Mattie saw what happened that day as you were leaving the stables astride Ginger. You tried to run Kate down."

"Oh Mattie, Oh Kate! Well you can have the both of them, since you've always cared more about everybody or anybody or *thing* , beside your own wife!" Judith pushed the lid to her designer luggage shut with force. She swung around to slap Joe, when he came near her, his intent to hold her and make her listen to reason and his declaration of love. She pulled away with solid strength and struck Joe across the face. Joe grabbed her, holding her against his chest, her arms pinned to either side of her strong, slender body.

"I love you Judith, and I always have, I don't know what has changed you from that bright girl I married, unless you were hiding who you *really* are for the first few years of our marriage..." The hurt and anger burned in Joe's gray eyes...I've begged you seek help, I know Pastor Phillips has offered to help you with whatever it is that seems to take you to dark places...because... I ...don't know how to help you...?" Joe faced his own feeling of helplessness and released her. "I'm sorry I've failed you, Judith... I really am sorry..." Joe said sadly. Judith turned away tears flooding her face. She shook her head, picked up her luggage and stomped out of her home and drove away.

"Where she going?" Mattie asked quietly, tears in her eyes for the both of them. Joe turned away from the window and heaved an exhausted sigh. "She wouldn't say, but I'm sure it's to her mother's in Kansas City.

"Is she coming back?" Mattie whispered.

"She didn't say, and I didn't ask. I think I'm done, Mattie. It's not just her cruelty to Kate, it's just Judith herself, the way she is with me...with everybody. I think I'd rather risk another stint in Afghanistan!"

"Well, let's give it up to God." Mattie encouraged. We might think praying is the last thing we need to do, but it should be the first." Mattie said, hugging her big, strong nephew whose heart was broken...again. Joe bowed his head, and Mattie prayed.

Kate recovered quickly at the Veterinarian's Clinic, the main danger was dehydration, but the seventy-two hours of confinement in such tight, cramped quarters had a lasting effect on Kate, one the doctor recognized, as well as Joe, and all who were close to Kate. With all the loving attention she got from Joe and Mattie, Flax Robinson and his boys, and the Jenkins. Kate finally came around to her old happy self, but she was *different.* Koki Spangle phoned, and insisted Joe fly Mattie out to visit her for a few weeks. "Sis is over-due a vacation with me, Joe." She said. "I expect you to spend some time with me as well, Son...But, listen, I know what would do you the best of good, and that's a visit with your cousin, Janice, and the children. I hear that Levi is away on business somewhere?"

"That's right, Mother. Levi's testing ground for a new store..."

"My, my, don't you and Levi have enough of those by now?" Koki lamented.

"Joe laughed. You're probably right, Mother. "Have you any word from Judith, dear?"

"Three months now, and nothing. I've asked my lawyer to start divorce proceedings."

"I dare' say it's for your own good, son, though I'm sorry for the girl." Koki said kindly.

"Thanks, Mother. Well Mattie and I will be down there soon...Is it ok to bring Kate?"

"Oh sure, Joe, she'll love the beach and the ocean...wish you'd move out here Joe!"

"I'm invested pretty deep right here, sweetheart...I do love the land and my dabble in the cow business...Listen we'll be driving if we bring Kate...She's a little squeamish since...her ordeal, but I hope she will make the trip with Mattie and me... Otherwise we'll take the Cessna."

"Wonderful, just be careful Joe..." "Sure Ole' Girl, you know I will. Love you!" Joe said good-bye to his mother, feeling better than he had in months, and Mattie's anxious excitement about the trip was sweet entertainment. He'd have to take her to Branson to the Mall for new clothes, and a make-over at the fancy salon there, a little touch up for her hair...Dear Aunt Mattie, she never asked for anything, and the good salary he paid her lay in the Bank rarely touched. Mattie was just happy having someone to take care of that, was just her way...

Joe was at a loss and more than a bit perturbed at his *Ladies.* Mattie refused any sort of "high-fluttery", (as she called it), at the Branson Mall, and Kate refused to step one paw inside the Van. *Females!* At least Mattie loved to fly in the Cessna, and was raring to go, as soon as Joe had Kate taken care of. Kate would stay with the Jenkins, and the Robinsons boys while on the job, and Joe made a three day practice run of the arrangement before he and Mattie left for the Florida Keys. Kate loved Mrs. Jenkins, and Mr. Jenkins was a laid-back pleasant man that would be a good temporary Master for Kate. He and Mattie bid Kate good-bye at home, to let her know they were coming back, while the Jenkins waited to walk her the two miles down the road to their place...Kate would ride in the open Jeep with Joe, but that was the only transport she'd tolerate, though she used to jump in back of the Joe's pick-up truck without a second thought. Joe didn't like the boundaries Kate had set for herself; he liked the free-wheeling, no-fears Kate...

Strange, that Kate would make him think of Judith…how free and fun and loveable she was when they first married, and then the sudden and permanent reversal. Judith refused to fly, or take long car trips, though she had no fear of driving. She would ride her horse Ginger like a professional, jumping fence, and narrow streams and hedges, and racing her like she was in competition with the wind, but she seemed bound with some puzzling condition, though the through physical and mental tests she'd gone through found her to be sound in body and mind. Mattie, of course, recommended God. They rarely attended church, and Joe, though from a Catholic family on his father's side, had not been to Mass in years. He'd made a commitment to Christ, but his involvement with the church was not a big part of his life, although he supported the church generously. He had a great respect for Pastor Phillips at the Community Christian Church, but was disappointed when *the man of the cloth* could not help his wife, yet he was aware that Judith hardly gave the man a chance. Joe shook his head to get the thoughts of Judith and her troubles off his mind.

It was a beautiful autumn day in September when Joe and Mattie left for Florida pleased that Kate seemed contented with the Jenkins and the trio of young men that helped their father with managing the farm, and caring for the dairy cattle. "I don't think she's plans on missing either one of us!" Mattie exclaimed as they drove away.

"Yes I noticed." Joe said, "and I might be a little offended except I'm proud of the fact that Kate is confident we're both coming back."

"Well she's had plenty of experience in your leaving and retuning." Mattie said.

"Yes, but there was always you…someone at the house with her." Joe said, amending speaking of Judith, when she wasn't a person Kate nor he wanted to come home to- truth be told.

"Well she's a grown-up now, no puppy you can fit in your pocket." Mattie remarked.

"Kate was never a pocket pup!" Joe laughed.

"Well I guess she just seemed so compared to the 120 pounds of her now!" Mattie laughed. Mattie changed the subject to their trip and Koki, and Joe's going on to visit Janice and the children in Plum Creek, Pennsylvania after a few days with his mother.

"I love my job, keeping up with the stores, and the employees, providing jobs… but I'm never more at peace than when I am with my family." Joe told Mattie. It was heart touching, since Joe wasn't one to speak his heart very often, but his love for family was always apparent to Mattie. "You're a wonder, Joe, a real wonder." Mattie said looking out the windows of the Cessna at the cotton fluff clouds against a beautiful blue sky

12. CHAPTER ELEVEN

The Jenkins were quiet shocked when Judith Spangle showed up at their door one evening, demanding custody of Kate. Mrs. Jenkins who had answered Judith's knock, invited her in and said she'd have to speak to Mr. Jenkins about Kate.

"I'll fetch Mr. Jenkins she said. "He's out in the shop working on something for the tractor." Judith nodded and settled back in the big high-backed chair, crossing slender legs encased in keen-high boots, her snug fitting skirt shifting high above her knees. Mrs. Jenkins looked away, adjusted the set of the collar of her neat shirt-waist dress and hurried out back.

"You better be careful with her, Clay, Lyla Jenkins warned her husband. She seems itching for trouble, and don't let those exposed thighs of hers make you do something you'll regret!"

"You're making a mountain out of a molehill, Lyla. I'll just explain that Joe left us in charge of Kate, and we can't turn her over to anybody but Joe, simple as that."

Clay Jenkins said with a period nod. "You hope…" Lyla said, which got a scolding look from her husband. Clay Jenkins turned and patted Kate on her big head.

"I'll be back, Kate. You stay put, darlin, he said, and then took hold of Lila's elbow, pushing her ahead. "What am I your protection against *fall-out?*" Lyla said freeing her arm. "Naw, I'm just feared I might gaze upon Mrs. Spangle's legs." He snickered a laugh, but quickly set his face in non-negotiable mode as they entered the living room.

"Lo' Mrs. Spangle." Mr. Jenkins gave a respectful nod of his graying head. "Nice to see you. You're looking well." He said and avoided looking past her eyebrows.

"I've come to take Kate home. There's no need for your help now that I'm back home." Judith said quickly.

"Well you see, Miss; Joe left Kate in mine and my wife's care until he and Mattie get back here, and we have to follow through on that, you understand…"

"I can get the Sheriff if I have too." Judith said one leg over her knee pumping like she was trying to go somewhere sitting down.

"Well if you have too, but he'll tell you same thing I just did. Our business is with Joe Spangle. You can call Sheriff Putter on the phone there if you like." Mr. Jenkins offered pointing to the land-phone on the lamp table next to where she sat.

"I can do that from my own phone." Judith snapped as she rose from the chair and walked toward the door. "I'll be back." She said glancing back at the couple who smiled and nodded pleasantly.

"She's a mean one, Clay." Lyla said shaking her head. I heard that Joe has filed for divorce so she aint got no business back on the farm."

"Well she might." Clay replied. "Well then I think you ought to take Kate and go off fishing. Nobody but God knows where you're old fishing shack is."

"Sounds like a plan, woman, you want to come with us?"
"I'd better stay here just in case the Sheriff gets involved, but I'll fix you and Kate a basket of food to take with you."
" Thanks woman. I'll take my old jeep. Kate will ride in an open air vehicle at least for Joe she will, and if not with me, she'll just trot alongside." Clay Jenkins shrugged.

"Let me talk to her if she refuses to ride, Clay."

"Fine Madam, Master *of Persuasion*." Clay Jenkins said a little irritated at any delay. "I have to fetch my fishing rods, and Kate. Meet you in the driveway, lady." He replied as he headed out the back door.

Lyla Jenkins almost dropped the picnic basket of food when she stepped out on the front porch and found Clay's old army jeep blocked by an enormous black pickup-truck. The headlights of the truck were blinding poor Clay who had his arm shielding his eyes.

Kate simply jumped down from the Jeep, putting herself out of the bright beam of the headlights, her growling snarl barely heard over the running engine of the big truck.

"What in the world!" Lyla exclaimed, squinting to recognize the figures behind the powerful glare. Judith Spangle stepped out of the glare and walked across the yard to the edge of the porch. She was in jeans and western boots, her thighs tightly covered in denim. "I told you I would be back." She said. I've come for my husband's dog."

"Like we told you Mrs. Spangle, our business with Joe's dog- is with Joe." Lyla said, while she tried to think of what to do next. "I take it the County Law was of no help to you?" She was vying for time, when a man burst out of the light and stood beside Judith Spangle. He held a dog mussel and a heavy chain leash in one hand, his other hand waving in impatience. He was a young man, powerfully build, dressed in black; a knitted cap rolled and perched on the crown of his head.

"Look lady, we don't want any trouble, just hand over Miss's Spangle's dog…"

Lyla didn't know how it happened but Clay put the old Jeep in grinding gear and yelled for Kate to "Hop on!" and squeezed passed the giant duly at a good speed. The young man tuned about at the sound of the grinding gear's and ran toward his truck, while Judith taken by the unexpected seemed immobile. "Don't just stand there like stupid!" He yelled as he climbed in his truck on the passenger side, leaving the door open for Judith. Judith sprinted across the yard boarded the truck as it back out of the driveway catching the door and slamming it shut when it slowed a second for the forward gear. Lyla ran into the house and called Sheriff Putter, then sank into the chair beside the phone in fear of her husband killing himself in a get-away-chase. He couldn't out run that big duly truck…or could he? Clay had earned Military Honors, and Metals for his driving abilities during the Vietnamese war, the Government had given the Army issue Jeep to Clay, retiring it in his custody…But Clay was not young anymore…she worried. And what might that muscle-bound blond-headed bully due to poor Clay when they caught up with him? Lila's heart was pounding so loud she could hear it. She jumped when she heard the siren of the Sheriff's car coming close and ran out the door to the end of the driveway. She did not want to waste a minute of time. "They went that way" She yelled and pointed when the Deputy lowered the passenger window. "Hurry!" She cried, to deter them from stopping for any more details than she'd given frantically over the phone. The Deputy nodded and they sped off siren blazing.

Clay knew he could not out run the dually on the road. He'd have better chance in the rough terrain of the woods. He knew ever path, tree, rock and gully like the back of his hand, and he led the big duly purposefully into the woods. When the bright lights came upon them Kate bailed out of the Jeep and headed deeper into the woods, the path wide open to the right…"Kate!" Clay Jenkins hollered as loud as he could, but Kate was like white lighting that became a blur in the big headlights. Clay tried to wave the big dually down, but his frantic arms were ignored, and he dropped his head his shoulders shaking when he heard the too-late braking just before the thunderous crunch of metal and glass as the big truck careered down the steep rocky cliff to the water below.

Clay pulled himself out of his fear and grief when he heard the sound of the siren in the distance. He quickly backed and turned his Jeep around and headed for the paved country road. He came to a stop at the road side turned the Jeep, and came to a sudden stop, as he tore off his white shirt and stood in the head highs of his Jeep waving his shirt his old eyes weeping.

The Sheriff was immediately on his car-phone setting up the Rescue Team as Clay spilling out instruction of where the crash went down. "Can you get yourself home, Clay?" Sheriff Putter asked with a broad hand on Clay Jenkins shoulder. "Lyla is frantic about you…"

"That big ole' dog of Joe Spangle's might have gone over the cliff… or been run over…her name's Kate…"

"I'll see to her." Bill Putter said as he walked Clay to his Jeep.

"I'm awful sorry about those two young people…Sheriff…I wasn't intending nothing like this…" Clay swiped at the tears he felt escaping his old brown eyes that had seen a lot of tragedy .

"They had no business with you, Clay. They brought this on themselves." Sheriff Putter said. "Now you go on home to Lyla, she's really worried about you." Clay gave a sorrowful nod and drove back down the road and home to Lyla.

Ω

The Rescue took hours into the night. Judith was found on the bank of the deep wide spread of Serenity Creek, alive, but critically injured. The divers recovered the body of the blond young man, Rick Mason, a former Security Guard at the Spangle Ranch. He died on impact as he nor was Judith secured with the seatbelts. There was no sign of Kate.

13. CHAPTER TWELVE

"You were right, Joe. Kate risked her life to save me." The words were spoken softly and almost breathlessly as Judith smiled. Tears streamed down Judith's cheeks, her eyes full of light and peace. "Can you ever forgive me, Joe?...I was...really messed up..."

"Of course, darling. Don't worry about the past, just get well and come home...to me!" Joe soothed her forehead, gently pushing back damp strands of her dark hair. Wondering in grief why it took such a tragedy for them both to realize their failures. His voice was quiet and low, breaking as he tried to keep control, but his tears mingled with hers. "I love you Judith, I've always loved you..." Judith smiled. I think I'm just now learning about love, Joe...Pastor Phillips...he...awakened me to Christ...I am all right now, Joe...I love you too..."

"I'm all right now, Joe..." These words were somehow sweeter than her last. Joe broke down completely, his body shaking with the weight of his sorrow. Pastor Phillips standing outside the curtained intensive care bed with the doctor came quickly leaning over Joe's weeping body and embracing him. This is not the end, Joe. You and Judith will have an eternity together." He said, smiling through his tears.

Two weeks later, when the brilliant leaves of fall covered the ground, and celebrated life with their exhilarating color, Joe took Kate to the lovely stone-fenced graveyard and stood before the grave stone, and sat their wedding photo on the leaf covered grave. Kate sniffed it, and gave a mournful whispery cry, looking up at Joe with sad eyes. "Yes, Judith is gone." Joe stooped and leaned on his heels an arm across Kate's shoulders. You saved her in more ways than you can know, Kate. Joe tried to explain. "You did good

Kate! Good girl!" Joe said rustling Kate's recently groomed coat at the swift and gentle hands of Lyla Jenkins.

Kate gazed up at Joe remembering the flowers she'd dug up in Judith's garden, when she was just a pup, and how she helped Joe to put them back into the earth...With Judith, her Mistress, Kate realized she'd done something good too... *She had done what she had to do...*

It had taken all of her courage to jump in the water after she'd scrambled carefully down the side of the thirty- foot Cliff. She dreaded the weight of her thick coat when it was wet, something Kate tried to avoid, but tolerated when necessary. Kate had seen the door fly open just at the big truck hit the rock side of the cliff on the other side of the creek. She saw Judith's body plunge into the water, and *something* propelled Kate into the water after her; Kate's strong canine jaws clamping down on the back of Judith's shirt and bringing her to the bank of the creek. Kate had stayed with Judith, licking the side of her face, whimpering, as she looked up the side of the cliff expecting Clay Jenkins to appear to help and when he failed to appear, she continued to stay with Judith licking the her hands, her cheek… until humankind help arrived with noisy vehicles and bright lights. Kate ran and hid in the scrub brush. She watched as a flat bed on ropes came down, and three men scaled the cliff. They talked and worked quickly and soon Judith was lifted up and taken away. Kate ran away after that, taking the path of the winding creek back home; where she hid amongst the breeder cows for days, disappearing here and there when she caught the scent of Flax Robinson or any of his sons, and never came out of hiding until she heard Joe's whistle and call. Her heart had never felt such relief and Joe had never needed her comfort as he had now.

Kate stayed hid in the garden when all the humankind came to the farm. She knew that Mistress Judith had died. Her canine senses had *expected* that she would not survive, and Kate had felt sorrow for Joe, and the humankind that came, all feeling and expressing grief for her Mistress' *going*. She'd come out of the garden with Joe as he re-acquainted her with her first humankind family, the Coats. She recognized them all, but her heart seemed to suddenly become light at the sight of her *Little Masters*.

They all had gone, all the people, the humankind, and once again it was only Joe, and Mattie, The Robinson's and the Jenkins, and it seemed better than before, yet a little sad.

Now she was in a beautiful place of trees and flowers remembering all the recent events, her heart happy with Joe. She smiled, and raised up to her four-legged height, gave a bark and a playful run and jump, beckoning Joe from the gravestone as the brilliant leaves fluttered around her paws and in the air.

14. CHAPTER THIRTEEN

The Gathering

Mattie and Koki had taken a commercial flight to Branson, a limousine waiting their arrival and driving them to Joe's small ranch. Joe had flown his Cessna home from Plum Creek, and Janice, Levi, and the children came the next day by plane. Later Joe's Aunt Emma Mae, and Uncle, James Kent arrived, and many of Joe's Store managers and employee's came to Judith's funeral and to offer Joe sincere sympathy for his loss. Mattie, Koki and Emma Mae Kent had little to do but direct Flax Robinson and his son's in setting up tables on the terrace and the colorful leaf-strew lawn for family and friends and neighbors to dine with them for their was not room inside the house for all their guests. The great and delicious amounts of food came from nearby neighbors, the Community Church, and Caters came from Branson, courtesy of Joe's business neighbors and friends. The out-pouring of love seemed to Joe to come from Judith's *renewed heart,* as well as from all the gracious family and friends, and through them straight from the heart of God.

Joe Spangle, brokenhearted and distraught with grief had called his mother-law, Susan Clark, in Kansas City and told her of Judith's tragic accident and the internal injuries that resulted in her death. He also told her of Judith's death-bed conversion of Faith in Christ, which seemed beyond her comprehension. She declined coming to her daughter's funeral though Joe offered to pay her plane fare and offered her accommodations in his home or a hotel if she preferred. They were truly strangers. Judith was not close to her mother, and had never expressed interest in having her visit at the ranch. Her father was deceased, and her two brothers had disappeared from her life when she was a teenager.

It was no wonder Judith was so alienated and bitter, and the superficial love she had for Joe was not enough to keep her heart in good stead…Joe again found comfort in Judith's last words…"I'm alright now, Joe…I love you…"

It was incredible even to Kate, but she recognized her little masters, (although little no more), because of their scent…and though they had grown as she had grown…their features were much the same. Emma with her ready smile, and freckles across her pert nose, and Theo, with dark russet hair, and long length like Levi.

"You're still the best dog in the whole wide world!" Eleven year-old Emma Mae Coats exclaimed as she walked with Kate in the Garden after all the guest had left. She laughed, knowing she still sounded little girlish about Kate. "You look just like your momma, Shaggy. Shaggy was killed, ran down by a drunken old man. He went to jail for a little bit, but that didn't bring Shaggy back…that was real hard on us all…especially with you gone with Uncle Joe…" Emma informed as if Kate could understand every word. Either way, it was good to have this talk with *little-girl* – Kate.

"Hey, Em' are you in here?" Theo called from the garden's gate.

"Yes, I'm back here with Kate."

"Where else?" Theo said out loud, and shook his head at the predicable. He walked toward the back of the garden, and found them next to bushes of pink roses still in bloom. "Are you going to bawl your eyes out when we have to leave Uncle Joe and Kate, like when you were little?"

"I might." Emma said, unashamed of her sympathetic and compassionate nature.

"Well I think you might want to grow up a little, be strong for Uncle Joe. Don't make him any more sad than he is." Fifteen year-old Theo advised.

"You sound just like Mother." Emma said, giving Theo a strange, but admiring look.

"Well come on then… "Theo said both pleased and

embarrassed. " Uncle Joe wants to feed Kate before she goes out to the pasture with the calves."

"Theo, do you think Aunt Judith *really* planned to kill Kate?" Emma whispered, not sure of how much *English* Kate actually understood.

"No one knows, Em, but we must forgive Aunt Judith if she did intend to harm Kate."

"We really didn't know her very much…but Momma say's she was very nice, but then something happened to her…like something bad got into her heart…I'm sorry she died…" Emma sighed, unable to understand it all.

"Me too." Theo said and put his arm across Emma's slender shoulder. "The great thing is that Aunt Judith accepted Christ Jesus into her heart before she died. We can know that she is no longer troubled, and she's with Jesus in Heaven." Theo explained.

"Now you sound like Pastor Phillips!" Emma said looking up at Theo. "Where is my big brother and what have you done with him?" They both laughed as Theo whistled for Kate to follow them to the back porch where Joe waited with her grub.

15. CHAPTER FOURTEEN

The twenty-eight days of February seemed twice as long, the freezing weather keeping them indoors except for necessary duties outdoors. Angle kept busy with cleaning out closets, and changing out the upstairs guest bedroom for her Art Studio, (the heavy work done by younger friends) as she and Ken exchanged his loft for the master-bedroom downstairs, because of his untrustworthy knee-joints. Annie Marie, the charming, and lovable Spaniel, who did not mind grooming of her lovely wavy white coat with its Ivory undertones, followed Angel's every step, trying her best to be helpful, returning old shoes to the closet, Angel was organizing, and everything else, that had been tossed into piles, for either the trash or for the Help Center in town. She called for Ken to whistle Annie down stairs, but when he didn't answer, she came down stairs ordering Annie Marie to take the lead. Jack was at the living room window looking out, and Angel could see from the stairs what held the interest of her intelligent, and handsome black Labrador. She saw Ken tossing fresh hay into Katie Love's big blue Tepee. The old hay piled and placed in the burn-drum. Katie stood watching her head moving in synchronized nods to Ken's lifting hay from the bale with the three pronged fork, and spreading it over the vinyl ground covering beneath her shelter. The hay had to be dry and deep, the old camp- comforter on top for protection against cold wind, and for added warmth. Angel hurried to the laundry room, grabbed her fiber-filled winter coat from its hook and boots on the floor beneath and headed out the front door, pausing only to instruct Jack to keep Annie downstairs near him.

"Mind if I help, Babe?" Angel grinned and broke up the hay bale more and provided the raking while Ken tossed the hay. "Sure! Ken grinned back at her and when she wasn't looking tossed a good bit of hay over her head. Angel brushed at it with a fighters snarl, and in deep-voice with pretended wrath said "You dirty rat!" Ken laughed at her mobster imitation, and her failed effort to crown him with hands full of hay. "Thought you came out to help and you're just goofing-off the job!" Ken teased. "Time and a half, Bud, and my clock is ticking." Angel retorted. They both laughed and returned to the job, Katie Love watching the humankind play, with laughter in her eyes, but she did not join in as in the early days.

As times before, when the job was finished, they let down the Tent at the open side and went inside the tent calling for Katie to join them, but she stubbornly refused. They came out and loaded the dirty hay in the wheel barrel and hauled it to the burn drum and set a match to it ignoring Katie Love, giving her, her freedom to choose, but she lay in the snow just outside her big blue Tepee. Finally they lifted the tent drops leaving the side open, and Katie Love let herself in and settled in the fresh hay beneath the comforter. Ken and Angel put away the forks, rake and wheel barrel in the barn and returned inside the house, while Katie's eyes and nose peeked from hay and comforter and viewed the white-covered ground and the blue, blue sky.

Ω

It was a perfect winter's night for hot soup and fresh baked cornbread and later steaming cups of coco and bakery cookies, and for Angel to read aloud from a World War Two mystery novel. Ken listened from the comfort of his easy chair, enjoying the rise and fall of Angel's voice as she read, and the subtle nuances when she gave voice to the characters. Annie drowsed, snuggled on the sofa with Angel, while Jack attentive, sat at her feet like a soldier. Angel couldn't help a looking up from her book to see if Katie Love was standing outside the big window looking in with her opened mouth grin as in the early days, when Sugar was with them and always at her feet next to Jack. She had drifted off her reading, and Jack who seemed to be really into the story gave an anxious whimper, and Angel smiled at him and went back to her animated reading, not missing Ken's *knowing* when he tried to hide a quick glance at her and then toward the window.

Outside under the evening stars Katie Love was comfortably nestled in the hay, the thick padded nylon comforter a good brace against wind and cold, and Katie with her layers of thick tendril hair was contentedly warm. The snow was still soft beneath its crunchy cold and the evening wind was mild. Katie loved to listen to the crackling tree branches and the wispy-movement of the Squirrels that found cozy shelter in hollow places in the Oak trees. She loved the pungent smell of the Fur trees in the yard, and the Pines out back and in the pastures. The wind, soft or strong, seem to carry a sweet song of memories… This day in particular reminded Katie of the peaceful, and very happy times with Joe Spangle after Judith was no longer with them.

$$\Omega$$

Kate had done her best to comfort her friend and master, Joe, but his grief was strong for a long time, but he was grateful of Kate's companionship and love, and always demonstrated his affection for his Canine friend. But then it happened, the gradual return of happiness and pure sweet joy of just being alive, and blessed by God and nature, and Joe was out and about with renewed energy, but he stayed close to home.

Kate had slept at the foot of Joe's bed for a long time, but when he was well again she was ready for the outdoors both day and night. She did however wonder in and out when *she* was needy of a bit of extra companionship and encouragement from Joe, although Kate herself found nothing amiss on the farm *or in her world*. All was well. It was just that far-off sixth sense that kept her heeling Joe everywhere he went.

She might have been just a little bit jealous when Joe began bringing Greta Martin out to the farm. Kate remembered Greta from her flying days with Joe. She had always accompanied Joe when he went to the Airport office for his flight schedule or other business, and Greta was always pleasantly affectionate towards Kate, and sometimes gave her tasty treats, however, Kate was Joe's focus, though he was friendly and respectful of Greta, who he considered *just a kid*. But Kate was now a young adult Canine, and in three years, Greta was no longer "just a kid" in Joe Spangle's eyes. Joe had always admired Greta's pilot skills, and they had the love of flying in common, and Greta Martin, with her wholesome personality was easy to like. Mattie cooked special meals for them, and they in turn would do the cooking, and Mattie acting so surprised when it turned out to be more than just edible! Greta and Joe played a bit of baseball out on the vast front lawn, and Kate was outfield chasing down the balls batted high and wild, and she even caught one of Greta's fly-balls and it felt like she'd bitten into a rock! Her jaws ached for days afterwards, and when Joe realized what was wrong discarded the hard-ball for a tennis ball. Those were wonderful days, and Katie had come to love Greta as much as she knew her friend and master Joe loved her.

The wedding, two years after Judith's death, was in a beautiful country church near Greta's parents' home in Kimberling City. The sun- spring day was perfect, without wind and rain to dampen or muss-up the bride's lovely dress and hair arrangement or require any quick impromptu changes of the Wedding Day Plan. The wedding was for close friends and family, but Greta seemed to have an abundance of aunts, uncles and cousins, both her parents and two sets of grandparents. Joe had his darling mother, Koki, his most special aunt, Mattie, endearing cousins Janice, Levi, Theo and Em; and his dear aunt Emma May and James Kent. There were the Robinson's, and the Jenkins, and a few of the Cherokee Spangles from Oklahoma. The little church was spilling over, the double doors wide-open for a few other unexpected guests…But Katie, called *Kate* back then, was shampooed and fluffed and perfumed, and with a flower in her hair was front-roll and center at the beautiful ceremony. She was situated in her place before the crowd gathered, and she had Mattie, and Lyla Jenkins feeding her favorite treats and keeping her calm as the church filled. But Kate remembered it all as a very good experience. She was a bit mesmerized by Greta Martin, the girl she usually saw in blue-jeans or corded slacks, now clothed in a long pearly gown with a crown of tiny flowers on her head, her long dark-blond hair cascading down her back in rippling waves that Kate related to the river's water skimmed by the wind. Kate had forgotten her fears of the past and was a proud member of the Wedding Party. Emma and Theo kept her busy with other young people after the ceremony, when everyone was out on the lawn and having lunch at many tables, with one long table laden with food flowers and a tall layered Wedding Cake…There was music, and laughter; talk and dancing, and plenty of children who thought *Kate* was "awesome!"

Joe and Greta were away for three weeks on their Honeymoon in Hawaii, but still checked on Mattie and *Kate* via Skype. Kate did not know just how Joe and Greta got into such a small box, but she didn't try to figure it out, she just accepted it. When they got ready they would come out of their little box and back to her in regular humankind size.

16. CHAPTER FIFTEEN

Changes

The air that Kate breathed seemed to be full of change. Joe and Greta worked on the interior of the house, Joe following Greta's instructions because he had no since of décor, was the happiest he'd ever been in his life. Greta replaced the formal look of the beautiful rock and wood home and gave it a saucy kind of country elegance, that Joe, though skeptical at first, begin to see something very lovely unfold as they painted, and replaced most of the furnishings. Greta found the "sitting room" in the forefront of the spacious master-bedroom, with oval shaped doors for privacy somewhat of a dilemma...or pretended that it was. Joe watched her scrutinize every inch of the nicely appointed room. It's twin silk loungers with a table between, expensive paintings by modern artist on the walls and the thick carpet over dark wood floors that extended throughout the house–the classic theme would be hard to replace.

"What will you do with *this* room?" Joe teased sure that Greta had run out of decorating ideas. He waited, and when she didn't answer right away, he begins to tap his foot as if impatient, but Greta would not be rushed. She creased her brow in thought, nodded her head at silent rejected ideas, and appointed and placed imaginary pieces of furniture with hand motions. Joe heaved a sigh and opened his mouth to interject one of his own opinions when Greta pivoted a turn, hands on hips; "What do you think of a Crib and Cradle theme?" She asked, her blue eyes sparkling with mischief.

"I don't know what that is....?" Joe stopped, his face taking on a light-bulb moment. "Sweetheart, Greta...you don't mean..." Joe looked ready to either pass out or burst, but simply gave a

Cowboy roundup holler when Greta shook her head rapidly in the positive.

"We're going to have a Kid, our very own Kid!" Joe yelled.

"Well I hope we're having a baby not a goat, Joseph Spangle!" Greta exclaimed as Joe picked her up and swung her around and around. Mattie came running, the outer double doors wide open to the sitting room, she cried, "What in the world is going on? You two been breathing too much wall paint?"

"No Mattie, Greta and me...Greta and I...we're having a Kid...a baby!" Joe laughed with joy.

"Well stop spinning the poor girl; I should think she's primed by now!" Mattie said grinning from one Irish ear to the other.

"Thank you, Mattie," Greta said a bit breathlessly, feeling a little tipsy when Joe set her on her feet. Kate had let herself in at the open backdoor when she heard the commotion returning from the pasture after a day's work with the calves. She pressed a paw on the glass storm-door and hurried toward the sound of voices and laughter, pausing at the sight of a three-way hug and stared curiously.

"Hey Kate, you're going to have a baby *Brother!*" Joe shouted. Greta shook her head at Joe's boyishness, while Kate barked her approval, at whatever it was that made them so happy, and scooted in for the hug fest.

Kate celebrated her fifth birthday the year little Joe Spangle was born, and she was his proud friend, body-guard, and slave to his every whim and whimper. Greta made Joe take Kate to Lyla Jenkins for a through grooming before she came home from the hospital with the baby. Kate was posted outside the nursery, and was given her first introduction on the terrace of the Master-bedroom. She was not permitted into the Baby's Nursery. It was a mildly brisk day in early September when the leaves were just beginning to reveal their autumn beauty. Joe escorted Greta, holding their son in her arms, gently out of the French doors and brushed leaves form the patio chairs. Kate waited looking on anxiously, a small, urgent whimper escaping her canine throat, while Joe seemed to be stretching out time, enjoying Kate's anxious self-control. Greta gave Joe a little elbow nudge. "Stop teasing her, Joe!" She whispered. Joe laughed.

"Oh come on over here and meet little Joe!" Joe said as he sat down. Kate gave a jump start, and Joe held up his hand. "Easy there Kate...calm down, remember you *are* a lady." He reminded her- as he did from time to time. Kate slowed and stepped lightly to view the tiny little addition to the Spangle family. Greta smiled nervously; stiffly protective of her first-born, though she trusted Kate. Kate had never seen newly born humankind, only little lambs and calves. She nodded her head from side to side, trying to get a fix on this new found treasure. She barked her happy approval, and Little Joe burst into a scream.

"*Great balls of fire!*" What's wrong with the Kid, Greta?" Joe exclaimed profoundly baffled that a kid of his could not appreciate Kate's loving approval.

The days seemed to fall into a happy and comfortable routine after a bit of frenzied acclaim from visiting grandparents' and the sets of great-grandparents. The rest of the family got acquainted with Little Joseph Andrew Spangle III, by way of Skype and snail-mailed photo's. The Spangle household had never been filled with such happiness and joy, and both the women and men of the family commented their delight with "What Greta had done with the place." It was a charming blend of woods and painted pieces of French Country furnishings, wispy curtains, and a white *wagon wheel, (Joe's idea),* that hung over the fireplace in the family room. The indoor plants, and hand-crafted tables and sofa pillows with splashes of colors, were a reflection of Greta's bright personality, with everything in keeping with her basic theme of blues and green, throughout the home. Most of the beautiful wood floors lay bare, only a good woven area rug in the family room that spread out before the hearth. The living room was more formal, but an easy comfort was always apparent in Greta's home make-over. It was a lovely, but not so fancy a home that one was afraid of mussing it up... In the Family Room, there were bookshelves and books, games and music, the game tables situated for serious games of Chess, and another for the little children to score for Go Fish or Operation or Checkers. Video Games and Big Screen TV were sentenced to the Basement game room, which was a favorite place for the older Cherokee Spangle and Martian Cousins to hang-out. Theo and Emma preferred the Chess and games of Bridge – the only thing saving them form *Nerdsville* was their cool dance moves resigned to the basement as well - the grandparents calling out "Now don't you kids hurt yourselves…!"

The next year, in the late days of summer, Little Joe was riding bare-back on Kate's well-padded back. Little Joe grasped little hands-full of Kate's long hair, laughed and giggled while Greta watched from two feet away, her stomach showing *that* melon roundness, and Joe when he was home, ran the video camera.

"Giddy-up Ka-tee!" Little Joe called in his toddlers voice, nudging Kate with his little feet, like his daddy taught him to do when he rode his miniature Shetland horse. Nothing was too good for Joe Spangle's boy! He had miniature trucks, cars, and an assortment of sports equipment all stored in the shed Joe had built to store it all. Greta finally put her half-pint size foot down, and forbade Joe to buy another thing beside necessities for Little Joe. "Don't' spoil him Joe", she insisted. "Teach him about the land, and the cattle, teach him to *Work*, Joe!" She begged.

Joe laughed. Work? The kid hasn't celebrated his *first Birthday yet!*"

When Little Joe was almost two years old a little bit of blond competition came into his life. Her name was Chloe Lane, a namesake for Joe's beloved Aunt, Mattie Lane Smyth, with his mother's blessings. Joe again was blessed to tears, something so touching to both Mattie and Greta that such a tough and rugged looking man could weep unashamedly in gratefulness and love for his children and their mother. " Ka'tee! Ka'tee" Katie Love heard the echo of Little Joe's baby voice in her dreaming… But it was Angel calling "Katie Love, Katie Love", and she rose for her breakfast feed, and a fresh drink of water, and her usual daily visit with her Mistress.

The next day, Thursday the Twelfth of February, Katie Love woke from her dreams at the yapping barks of Little Sammy. It had been over a week since their last trek into the woods, and Katie feeling the need for exercise rose up out of the hay and shook her stiff aching body and headed down Elm Tree Road with her snappy energetic friend in the lead. Little Sammy held some mysterious *knowing* about Katie Love, that Katie did not understand, and wasn't at all sure she wanted to find out exactly what it was Little Sammy seem to know that had to do with *her*. They met Digger farther down Elm Tree Road, just before they took to the southeast pasture that would eventually take them into the woods. Katy saw her Master and friend, Ken, in the distance with the cows, but his back was towards her, and she did not disturb him or the cows with a loud barking greeting. She didn't want to see or hear his summons or see the sadness of concern behind his smile if she obeyed his call. She'd see him when she returned.

The dry cold had been much better for Katie's old bones, and she felt spry and adventurous today. Perhaps it was the wild meat of the offending Raccoon she'd killed the previous night. She had caught the mean little critter terrifying the horses, and the silly little fella thought he'd use the same tactic and watch Katie freak-out, but Katie was inflamed with his refusal to back-down and run away. She took him down quick and made a meal out of him, the first raw meat she'd tasted in a long while. Whatever it was, she was feeling quiet vigorous and decided she'd follow Little Sammy all the way into the woods and that particular spot he was determined for her to see and investigate with him.

They were less than a mile away from the Island shaped clearing when Digger's keen hound nose sniffed danger in the air. Katie Love knew that it was a small pack of wild dogs, and not the scent of wolves. Digger was nodding them back, his tail tucked and ready to fight, but wisely wanting to avoid any vicious conformation. They were peace-loving domesticated Canines, and were opposed to a tangle with their wild relatives, knowing they may not be the fighters their wild brothers were. Digger and

Little Sammy knew that Katie had lived in the wild for a time, but she was younger then, and her bones were agile and strong and her muscles solid…but now…well they were not sure of her strength, and neither one of them wanted to be hurt or have Katie taken down. Little Sammy opted to follow Digger's lead and high tail it in the other direction. However, it was too late, for the six-pack burst out of the brush and stood ground, ears laid back and tails tucked. They were itching for a good fight! Katie suddenly hit the ground rolling in a passive wiggling, with a happy grin, showing the pack she nor her friends were no threat to them. Digger and Little Sammy followed suite, hoping the tough looking wild-ones would not jump them while they were wiggling on the ground. The pack leader, a ragged, but healthy looking mix of mostly German Shepherd, raised his tail and let his ears stand. He gave a warning bark to Digger and Sammy who went ridged while the German sniffed out Katie. When the German Shepherd's examination got a bit drawn out and personal, Katie gave a friendly, but warning growl, and the pack leader stopped his sniffing but stood his ground. Katie roused herself up with a quick surge of adrenalin. She was taller and broader than the German and reared up like a horse to let him see her- even larger -and came to her fours quickly with a friendly smile. The German Shepherd seemed impressed with Katie, and allowed Katie to check him out. The other five stood back snarling, just waiting for a break in protocol, but when their leader was licking face with the big shaggy, they gave it up and took a lounging position waiting on their boss to be done with his flirting while they watched the two little intruders on their backs with feet raised to the sky.

17. CHAPTER SIXTEEN

At the junction where meadow met the crop of fur trees, Sammy led them into the clearing by a Pine and Fur -tree-lined narrow passage. As usual, Digger stopped short at the entry producing a small moan as if he were entering something eerie that his super senses could not determine, and that his sixth sense wanted to avoid. Katie Love feeling quiet stimulated and revived by the wild, raw meat of the previous night, and the successful negotiations with the German Shepherd mixer, along their way, was feeling spry and adventurous. Her confident stride, and canine grin blurred Diggers vague fears and he followed behind Katie who followed little Sammy into the shadowy pocket of woods. Sammy stopped short in the middle of the clearing as if to check his calculations of place. The three of them stood still as they waited for Sammy to reveal what it was he brought them here to see, but before he made his reveal, Katie Love saw something glint in the sunrays through the evergreen branches, and skeletal forms of great Oaks. She gave a little ruff that moved Sammy out of her path, and Digger backing up, as she darted to the winking object beneath the tall, fully branched Pine tree. She pawed and sniffed the metal, which seemed vaguely familiar, and noticed other odd shapes and pieces of the same metal, that was of a faded royal-blue color and the glinting silver. Something hit at Katie's subconscious, lingering a moment then escaping. She turned the dirt-stained rounded objects over and over as if to bring back that slice of memory, but her examination and Sammy's scratching in the earth around evergreen shrubbery was interrupted by the screeching scream of something up in the branches of the Pines. The three were seized with pure terror, bolted from the wide clearing and back down the narrow path to the meadow, with Digger in the lead. Bob Cat or screeching Owl, they did not hesitate to find out but ran a good long distance before they slowed, panting, and made their way back to Elm Tree Road in record time.

Katie Love saw her beloved friend and master, Ken in the windowpane. He stood near the window with his favorite mug filled with hot, minted coco. Katie barked and set her face in a happy canine grin, barked again and turned and quick-stepped and then back again with an inviting bark for Ken to come outside for a visit with her. Ken grinned back and gave Katie the thumbs-up sign. He put on his jacket and cap and stepped out the front door onto the porch. Katie met him there and Ken produced a big cookie treat and teased Katie to the cold, but dry out-door metal chair where he sat and gave her the treat. He let her sniff the hot minted coco.

"Want some?" he asked, but Katie shook her head refusing the offer, and licked the hand that had held the doggie cookie treat. "Sorry friend, I brought only the one cookie." Ken said as he rubbed her behind her ear. "Where have you been all day, Katie-girl?" He asked, truly wanting an answer or the details of what he already knew. She'd gone out into the woods with her little canine friends, and he wished he knew what kept them going back into that particular pasture beyond his land and Katie Love's home? It was land that belonged to someone else, and the person who owned it lived three or four miles away on the other side of the woods. If it were not for trespassing Ken would take the four-wheeler and follow the trio of canine trespassers and check out their obsession…he dared to do it anyway…but that was no respect to the land owner, and Ken shook his head in the negative at following his whim. It was just the little pack's natural instinct to roam, and easy enough for the *Country Canine pets to have the best of both worlds, the domesticated home, and land to roam and come home.* It wasn't the safest life, but freedom had its foes, and Ken knew that Katie Love and Friends could smell trouble a mile away. He moved Katie's dish of food and water next to his chair, and talked to her of their shared interests of the cows, and the horses and the challenges of the weather. "It's getting colder, Katie." Ken said when Katie had finished her late mid-day meal.

She looked up at him, and shook her great mass of hair, as if to say, I'm well prepared. Ken stood raised the garage door with the remote and invited Katie Love inside, but she barked a polite refusal, thanked Ken with a licking kiss of his hands and trotted off on a security check around the premises. Ken went inside via the garage and met Angel in the laundry room where she folded fresh bed linens.

"Katie's back home." He told her.

"Good." Angel replied. They both had to be satisfied with her on home ground if not *inside* the home on home ground. "I've got supper in the Crock. We can self- serve and watch that old movie with Nicolas Gage..." Angel suggested as she flipped and folded sheets.

"Sounds good." Ken said as he hung up his heavy jacket on the coat rack and hooked his cap next to it. I rewired that old lamp you bought at "Antiques", he said. "It's better than new." He bragged and grinned.

"I knew you could do it Babe. Thanks!" Angel said with a wink.

$$\Omega$$

Katie Love finished her security check and headed for the near pasture and the barn where the cows gathered to feed from the trough and would huddle inside the barn, the cold wind blocked out by the stacks of hay all around the walls, and the hay spread on the floor. It would drop to freezing tonight, and Katie *could* cuddle with the cattle, but she would not. The door would be shut and, Katie could not tolerate that kind of confinement. She'd go in while the doors were open and check out the barn for snakes, or other pests that might upset the plain and spotted cows, but then she'd return and bed-down in her Tepee. She was happy and content with her Tepee shelter, and was very proud of it, and of her friend who built it for her. The mooing of the Cows and the cawing of the Ravens were serene, comfortable sounds, a great satisfaction to Katie Love after the horrific ear busting screech of a feline predator...or was it just a screech-Owl? Katie had not seen or heard a Bob Cat since she was very young, but from time to time she'd heard the deafening sounds of the screech Owl, and the hair-raising scream she'd heard in the woods could have been the bird and not the cat, but Katie was not convinced of either or. The horripilation she'd experienced, her tangle of crinkling hair bristling, was like being struck with lightening. She came back into the yard as Jack was let out and they romped around together until Jack was let back inside, and Katie given hugs by her Mistress and Master before they closed the door and settled in for the evening. Katie would stay awake and alert, watchful that the terror of the woods did not find its way into the yard. *Guard The Yard!* Katie didn't have to be told, she knew her duty. She ran track around the circle drive and out on the connecting Elm Tree Road, and barked and growled loudly and viscously. Ken and Angel, startled by Katie's loud hellish growls, stood in the opened front door. "What do you make of that?" Angel asked Ken. "Not sure, but something's got her on the watch." Ken said. "Want to let Jack out, he will either confirm or calm Katie down."

"All right." Angel agreed.

"Jack, go help Katie." Angel said, and they stood aside as Jack ran out the door and to Katie who stood barking at the end of the drive. Jack joined her, pacing the edge of the road. Jack smelled nothing but the cedar smoke from chimneys, the evergreens and the usual scent of small game...nothing new or strange in the air on the ground. He grew quiet and nosed Katie to do the same. They stood side by side listening. *All is well,* Jack related to Katie, licking her face reassuring her that peace reigned. They came into the yard near the house, and parted company at the porch. Ken stepped out and gave Katie a whispered pep- talk, and thanked her for her good work. *All is well, Katie. All is well.*

Before night set in Ken layered more fresh hay into Katie Love's Tepee, after he'd bed down the horses and cows in the pasture barn. He built a wall of hay as tall as Katie would permit, which was as low enough that she could see the sky. The cold was becoming more intense, but it was a dry cold, and hardly any wind. Katie should be safe weather-wise, but Ken knew that Katie was taking risk she need not take, especially at her age. But wasn't that what the doctors told him about his knees? And did he heed their advice or warnings? To some extent yes, the very condition of joints limited one's *doings.* But what was limiting life's activities, but taking the spice out of living. It *might* be wise, but one needed to live longer with a purpose...for a purpose... Risk were all a part of life.... Were they not? Ken rationalized for himself and for Katie. He assured himself that both he and Katie knew when to come in out of the cold'....but he was more sure of his own timing than Katie was hers. He put up the hay fork, locked up the blue and silver barn and told Katie good night. She gave a puppy-like soft whimper when she wanted more of her Master & Friend's company. She listened for the low whistling of a melody that Ken always played for her, with his mouth, as she snuggled down, her face open to the sky, her clear night vision watching her friend disappear inside the walls of his house and Katie Love fell asleep.

It might have been the day's activities in the woods that provoked the nightmare, but Katie Love's historical dreaming had become something dark, and destroying...

It was a long hot summer, with spattering of electrified rain and farmer's fields were set on fire by heaven's match. Electrical storms were impromptu, many claimed without a hint of the usual warning sounds of thunder. It was the "Condition" of the Midwest, the Media Weather Reporters were saying. The animals could sense it coming; their built-in survival compass and weathervane did not need any humankind commentator to tell them what the weather would be like the next day or the next hour. The horses, dogs, cattle, and humans were staying indoors, and Joe and Greta relied on Kate for their weather report.

"It certainly is uncanny weather these days." Greta said with a long breath, tired of the humid heat and the electrical storms and staying indoors, *earthbound.* "I'd like to fly away somewhere...we should visit Janice and Levi and the children. There are no electrical storms back east." Greta said to Joe and Mattie, while her eyes were on her two diapered toddlers wrestling on the Persian rug in the family room.

Joe looked up from the game table as he took Greta's knight, and one of her pawns. "We can do that when we get a good day... Or if I'm tied up at the store, you could take Mattie and the kids ...."

"I don't want to go without you, darling. I'll just wait for that good day you've mentioned." Greta smiled.

"Well this isn't Cessna flying weather that's for sure. I think you're both grounded for a while." Mattie remarked, as she kept a Referee's eye on Little Joe and Chloe spotting their movies with her own untangling moves. Kate came in the back door noisily and with speed, and settled down on the rug in front of the cool stone hearth trying to act as if nothing unusual was going on. ... "And you know it's pretty bad out when you see Kate high-tailing indoors, when she'd rather be out under the sky than eat!" Mattie chuckled.

"We could take a commercial flight; they're cleared more frequently than the smaller, private planes. Dad won't let anybody up even when the Air Traffic Control clears us." Greta complained.

"Your daddy is a wise man, I'd say!" Mattie interjected as she called a foul on Chloe, which was ignored with a little giggle.

"Checkmate!" Joe called as he took Greta's last King off the Chessboard. Greta shrugged disinterested in the whole thing.

"Look at our little beasts, Greta!" Joe exclaimed. "We're supposed to be raising Pilots not Japanese Sumo wrestlers!" Kate barked at Joe's loud exclaim, and rose to nose in on the diapered duo.

When the weather turned back to *normal* summer weather the Spangles, Mattie, and Kate were outdoors dancing in the sprinklers, and having picnics here and yonder on the lawns, while Joe watched as he grilled burgers and veggies on the grill on wheels, sous table for the roaming picnickers. Joe would grab the sprinkler hose and kink it causing the hose to spasm like a Bionic snake, making the toddlers and the women-folk scream...

But there was another kind of scream Katie Love was remembering...and it wasn't one of tingling delight, but one that shattered glass.

Greta sent glass after glass flying off the long dining room table her screaming as erie and earth shaking as the terrible screeching of the big Cat. Katie startled awake as the forgotten memory came up out of its hiding, but her eyes were heavy with hibernation…and she fell back into vivid dreaming.

"My God, My God!" Mattie exclaimed in pain at what she witnessed. She come from the kitchen, a fresh white dishtowel over her thin shoulder. Mattie tried to hold Greta in the circle of her arms to stop her mayhem, but she could not be held. There were only the Robinsons' and the Jenkins' in the house, that had arrived early, but Joe's business associates, from Branson, and their wives had not yet arrived. It was a welcoming home dinner party for Joe. Kate, freshly groomed, with ribbons in her hair hurried to the playroom where Little Joe, and Chloe played, and closed the door. She would protect the little ones – the men were running towards the resounding screams.

"Miz' Spangle! Miz'Spangle!" Toby Robinson exclaimed running into the dining room. His younger brothers, Tad, and Billy, were on his heels. Flax Robinson blocked the door preventing the older couple, Clay and Lyla Jenkins from entering. "The boys and I will see to Miz' Greta." Flax told them quietly. He closed the double doors to the dining room, and his eyes could not believe what they saw. The beautifully set table with china and crystal was all awry, broken glass everywhere, and Greta, the quiet one, the strong, talented woman of The Spangle Ranch, was backed into a corner her eyes wide and terrified, herself as awry as the dining table, and as broken as the crystal that lay in chards on the floor. Mattie stood, leaning against the floor to ceiling window, as limp as a rag doll.

"Miss Mattie." Flax Robinson put a strong arm around her, and held her for her knees kept buckling. "Can you tell us what happened here…" Mattie looked up her old gray eyes wide and wild with grief. She handed Flax the cell phone. Someone was weeping…saying "My darling girl, my baby!"

"Hello?" Flax Robinson spoke nervously into the Smart Phone. "Who is this?"

"This is Bill Martin, Greta's father, is she all right?" The man said choking back his weeping.

"I believe she's in shock, Sir, and I need to tend to her...what happened?"

"Oh God, is that you, Flax?"

"Yes Sir...what...what's wrong?"

"It's Joe...uh...Joe went down...crashed the Cessna...He went down over in Douglas County...Tell my daughter I'm on my way...I'll bring the doctor, he lives nearby....keep her warm...give her a dose of whiskey if you have it...Flax.

Yes Mr. Martin, I'll take care of Miz Greta...but you hurry Sir...hurry!"

18. CHAPTER SEVENTEEN

Kate lay at the foot of Greta's bed her eyes sad. From time to time she would raise and walk to the side of the bed, licked the pale hand that lay limp along side Greta's sleeping body. A nurse sat beside the bed, and when Greta woke wild eyed the nurse would administer medicine into the clear plastic bag of nutrients being fed the patient via her veins. Kate whimpered her pain for Greta, and her own deep sorrow, as she watched the nurse go efficiently about her job.

It had been five days since the terror struck the house, and Greta Spangle. Joe had not returned, and there was a lot of weeping, and loud crying…Kate was told that Joe is gone, he's not coming back…Joe is dead…Kate did not understand all the words, but she knew something had happened to Joe because of all the sorrow around her. The humankind banded together, came and went, came and went, but Greta lay in her bed like a zombie – as if she had died too. Kate sensed Greta's feelings of loss, and being lost; because she felt lost without Joe too, and her sorrow was deep, but Kate had to stay calm for Greta and for the little ones and Mattie.

Flax Robinson and his boys came everyday with gifts of food, flowers, and cards. They had lost a wife and mother years ago, so they understood the shock and sorrow of losing someone so dear to one's heart. The weather turned cool after a summer rain and Mattie turned off the Air Conditioning and open-ended every window in the house. Billy Robinson came up outside the bedroom window, carrying a wooden chair and a guitar. Kate raised her head as he approached and then stood, staring out the opened window. Billy sat down, bowed his leg over his knee and begin to strum the strings of the instrument, then he begun to hum, then he sang softly…The words were cheerfully sweet, but

Billy seemed to labor over his guitar in serious concentration. Kate listened, her ears perked to the cording of the guitar, and Billy's soulful voice when Stella Martin entered the room, followed by Bill Martin, Doctor Walker, and Mattie.

"Nancy, Doctor Walker said to the Nurse who stood with he entered Greta's room. "Mrs. Spangle is off all medications. It's time for her to face reality, as tragic as it is for her…"

"Yes doctor." Nurse Nancy replied and immediately began dislodging the needle from Greta's arm, and removing the I-V bag to a safe container, and folding down the I-V's stand, until it was just a piece of moveable luggage. Doctor Walker thanked the nurse and said her duties with Mrs. Spangle were finished; and he and the family members thanked her sincerely.

Stella Martin sat where Nurse Nancy had sat reading when she wasn't tending to Greta's needs, and opened the lid of the small square box she carried and sat on her lap. There were ten vials of scented oils, all very poignant, and all designed to wake up Greta's mind to what is needed of her…The babies soaps, lotions, their favorite cookies, the smells of their toddler's foods, bananas, Melons, and peanut butter, and custard. Greta moved her head back and forth trying to avoid the poignant aromas, but Stella kept the process going quickly. Finally Greta slapped at the vials, but Stella quickly moved them out of her reach. She seemed to have become immune to them all, and closed her eyes in a lazy, lax way.

"I was sure the oils would wake her up…" Stella looked up at Bill defeated. "It's all right darling, she'll snap out of it…" Bill said tiredly. "Try this, Mrs. Martin." Mattie said and handed Stella a plump perfume bottle.

"Do call me Stella, Mattie, and Bill, well Bill. We're family are we not?" "Oh yes indeed…Stella." Mattie agreed. "What's in this bottle?" Stella asked holding it up and staring at the clear liquid. "Ammonia." Mattie said flatly. "Oh, I don't think so…" Stella began. "Give it a try Stella. It's not pretty, but its good and strong." Bill said.

"Well…I…" "Go ahead, its spill-proof Stella." Mattie encouraged. Stella Martin opened the little bottle and swam it under her daughter's nose. Kate vacated the room. Greta moved her head back and forth violently, and her eyes flew open. "What the devil is that?" She asked as she raised up in the bed and gave her family a disgruntled look.

"I think she's back with us." Mattie smiled. Praise be!"

19. CHAPTER EIGHTEEN

"Those damnable electric storms! Taking the life of such a good man as Joe Spangle!" Clay Jenkins lamented as he used his clean cotton handkerchief. Flax Robinson put his arm across Clay's skinny shoulder and pulled near. "Awful shame…a terrible loss for his family and friends…" Flax said agreeing with Clay Jenkins in their shared sorrow. "First time the lightning struck a building that we know of during this storm, and it had to be one of Joe's stores in Oklahoma City! Flax shook his head, sadness showing in his dark eyes. My boys are real broke-up about Joe's death, they loved him…we all did…still do…" Flax choked up, and looked up in the evening sky, then at Kate across the grass laying on Joe's grave.

Bill Martin, who stood next to Flax Robinson could hardly speak. He cleared his throat a few times before he had control of his own sufferings before he spoke. "The authorities are looking into the Oklahoma store fire…of course they always do, but seems they suspect arson, but nothing's been confirmed at this point. Joe wouldn't have been flying if it were not for that store fire…It was the lightening that brought down his plane, but it was the fire that put him to the sky. I sure tried to keep him grounded, but since the officials cleared him for flight I couldn't force him to stay on the ground…"

"Who but the good Lord knows the answers to such tragedy?" Flax said, and laid his free hand on Bill Martian's arm. One thing we do know… that we'll all be reunited with those gone on…what a day that will be!" Flax Robinson gave a joyful smile that was catching and the three men turned from waiting on Kate and headed to Bill's car.

"Kate will come home when she's ready." Flax said. Looking back over his shoulder as they walked down the lane to the parking area outside the graveyard where many dogwood trees were still in bloom. The wind whipped up suddenly and flowers from the trees showered over Joe's grave and Kate.

Ω

Katie Love felt the cold wind sweep over her bed of hay and camper-comforter. She woke with the same deep sadness she'd had when she was "Kate" and her beloved Friend & Master had gone away. Katie whimpered and moaned remembering, but she knew that she could not comfort Joe at his grave like she did lying near his bed and at his heels wherever he went, nor could Joe comfort her, but for the memories of their time together, and that it was the best …like it was now with her Friend & Master Ken, and Mistress, Angel. There's was the healing love from her wonderings with Ken and Angel…and from a lot of fear and mistrust of most humankind…Katie Love need not dream now to recall her past…she could recall the good times as well as the bad; and the terrible time when she was stolen and locked away…

A multitude of the Humankind came to Joe Spangle's *Going Away*. The first to arrive after Greta's and Joe's parents were Janice, Levi, Theo and Emily. The Cherokee and the Irish side of Spangle's gathered and filled many rooms at the Branson hotels. Many of Joe's Business friends and associates came for their great respect and love for their leader and friend. It was a large assembly that filled the pews in the Kimberly Community Christ Church, and services were also given at the little Country Church where Joe and Greta's Wedding took place. Greta still pale and wane from the loss of the *love of her life, her children's father, and the joy of Joe's presence to all who knew and loved him* sat still the, spidery dark vail of her hat, hid her pale face and swollen eyes.

… "To know Joseph Andrew Spangle was to love him." Those were only the beginning words of the beautiful, heartfelt eulogy that Levi Coats gave in the big church about the man he loved as a brother and best friend. Levi, who usually tried to control his emotions, let the tears flow as he gave his speech of love for Joe. At the end he gathered himself, and said "We need to weep for the loss of such a fine friend, husband, father and son…

but we also need to go on celebrating his life that touched so many in an endearing and positive way. Let us stand and give an old Irish send-off for a magnificent man of a great heart. The sound of many rising up gently thundered through the Church. "Three cheers for the Bonnie Irish Lad! Three Cheers! Three Cheers! Three Cheers!" The sound of blended voices rang out in the eco of the big church, and there were smiles behind tearful eyes of both big strong men, young and old, and women and children. The Church pianist played "Home Coming" as the weeping crowd filed out into the sunlight and a brisk breeze, a reminder of the approaching fall, and followed the white hearse to the beautiful walled gravesite in Gentry, with its marble-stone angles, and many Dogwood and Red Oak trees.

Ω

Katie Love remembered well following Greta and the little ones, Little Joe, and Chloe around indoors and outdoors at home on the Spangle Ranch in Gentry, and Greta sending her to Lyla Jenkins for her baths more often than she wanted to go, and more often than Joe had, but she did what pleased her young Mistress, and what gave her ready entrance into the house and their close company.

She watched as Greta lovingly took care of the flower garden and on that particular day, Lyla had just brought her home from her grooming. Lyla always like to stick a flower behind Kate's ear, twisting the stem around her freshly groomed tangles of white hair. It was often a pink rose as it was this day. Katie recalled laying on the terrace with Little Joe and Chloe bouncing around on her back pretending they were riding hard and fast to their Candy Store in Branson, their little voices hollering "Giddy-up Kate, Giddy on up!" Greta and Lyla looked on and chuckled, and praised Kate for her patience and tolerance. "Believe me if Kate didn't want them on her back she'd start shaking them off, and they *know* they'd better slide while she sits!" Greta told Lyla.

"Lyla laughed at Greta's telling, happy to see her laugh and smile again, though her pain of loss was still apparent behind her twinkling blue eyes. "May I help you weed or plant those Mums?"

Lyla asked stooping in the flower garden and then on her knees when Greta handed her a small garden troll. Lyla chuckled and thanked her, but her eyes lingered on Greta a question on her mind. "What?" Greta asked, lifting her slender shoulders.

"Oh, I have a silly question…" Lyla admitted.

"Go on with it then. I don't want you staring at me instead of the Mums." Greta said with a small teasing smile.

"Well…I've often wondered how you accepted living in the same house on the same land…and working the same garden …as well…the X-wife?"

"I think it made a big difference that all this, except this garden, was Joe's before he married Judith, and the fact that Joe didn't have a problem with the changes in the décor that I made… that was such a fun time for us…and that I got pregnant so soon, which we both wanted – that just made the place *our home* for the both of us. And as for Judith's garden, I've always considered it the reflection of who she really was…and she was someone Joe loved…I've only taken down the 'invisible fence' and extended the borders and used the natural rock like that on the exterior of the house…for fence- so to speak.

"You are an incredible woman, Greta Spangle!" Incredible!" Lyla exclaimed as she set the Mum's in the watered well she'd dug in the earth.

"Thanks, but I had some issues before I got there…but I think it was first my compassion for Joe, and then it just spilled over to Judith. I was so glad to hear that she left this earth Reborn in Christ."

"Indeed!" Lyla smiled. Lyla finished the last pat of moist potting soil around the pale yellow Mums, and noticed the tiny white flowering ground-cover just inside it's rock boarders.

"My, my what's this lovely border flower?" Lyla asked. "My Mother brought those and helped me - or made me help *her* plant them – just after Joe's funeral." Greta said, matter of fact. "They're beautiful, Greta! What are they?" Lyla asked.

"My Mother calls them "Whispering Hope." Greta smiled and shrugged, but tears welled up in her eyes. Lyla dropped her garden tool and leaned on her knees to embrace Greta. Kate watched from the terrace, gave a little shake and Little Joe and Chloe pushed off her back. They followed Kate to the garden where she came close and lay at Greta's feet. Little Joe, and Chloe danced and ran, toddling on the grass, their happy shrieks filling the late summer day with irresistible joy.

20. CHAPTER NINETEEN

It was just one of those days. A day Katie Love remembered as one longing for Joe, which prompted a visit to his grave. The leaves of the trees had turned their glorious autumn colors and many lay on the ground making a colorful path across field and lawn. Kate remembered the smell of the chimney smoke, the air brisk, the warm sun. She had taken her leave from the pasture and the young calves. She left Billy leaning against the barn, beside the door, strumming on his guitar, while Toby and Tad filled troughs with feed. "So long Kate…take it easy Kate…See ya mañana!" Those were the late afternoon farewells that Kate barked in happy reply. She had stopped at the house, because Mattie was on the back porch filling her double, stainless steel dish with meaty-smelling canine food and her water-bowl full of fresh well-water.

"Wipe your feet and come on inside for your treat when you're finished Kate." Mattie said and scratched her lovingly behind her ears. But Kate did not reply. She was going make an impromptu run to Angel's Rest which was about two miles from the ranch. Mattie gazed at her non-committal look, but shrugged…and said, "Don't be getting yourself too far from home, you hear me?" Mattie said. Kate snuggled her big head against Mattie. Mattie knew her about as well as Joe had, and Kate found it very comforting. She ate and drank and trotted across the lawn and the across the dirt and gravel road off the Spangle's front line. Kate noticed the red breasted Robins fluttering about the trees, and the Black Birds that lined the smooth fence line, and the few brave Sparrows' perched on the fence post here and there. A rabbit bound away from the fence as Kate approached, the horses seem to come close to welcome her, and why not? Had not some of Joe's buddies at the Martian Air Station called her a hairy horse.

And hadn't Joe told them she was much smarter than any horse... The memories...Joe's laughter, the shared play and games, the co-piloting the Cessna when she was still just a pup...sitting at his feet on the front porch while they both gazed at the stars, and Joe puffed and chewed on his cigar. Joe would talk about all sorts of things, funny things, serious things, sometimes sad things, but all of it was happiness to Kate. She'd cut across field, and yards until she was at the wide open gate of the Angel's Rest graveyard, with its rock pillars on either side aware that she'd have to leave before dark when the gates were closed and locked. The grounds keeper, Juan Garcia, made his rounds in a golf-cart his accented English calling "Closing Time, Closing Time, in a musical tone, so Kate felt safe if she fell asleep while she lay on Joe's grave.

And that's what had happened. She'd fallen asleep after a while, and not awakened until called "Miz Ka-tee –pooch, time to go". Kate roused herself and stood. "You go home now?" All of Juan's statements sounded like questions. Kate barked her answer and headed for the gate, while Juan followed on the golf cart his thumb ready on the Remote to close the gates form where he sat. Soon he would lock-up the little office and tool cottage and be on his way, the Remote ready at hand to open and close and lock the wide gates.

Juan Garcia heard the loud blistering noise of the truck out on the County Road and looked up his brow meshed in concern. "Be careful Ka-tee pooch!" he said out loud and then went back writing in his log-book, noting Ka-tee Pooch's visit to the Spangle grave-sight...arrival time and leaving time. It was all in the groundkeeper's log. He signed himself out, and left, looking for the hyped up truck he'd heard, but did not see. "Long gone." He said, and headed home to his wife, Juanita.

Ω

The noise sent Kate bellying under barbed wire her hair catching in the barbs and slowing her down, but she jerked free and stayed along the inside of the fence until the noisy truck, and the yelling humankind passed, the tail lights of the pick-up fading, along with the noise. Kate let herself back on the paved county road, her cross pasture was several kilometers away, and the road was smoother than the lumpy pasture. She found an open cow-rail and leaped over it on to the road, but she'd hardly readjusted her pace when the pickup came roaring out of another cow-railing gate on the other side of the road, and chased Kate down the road. She ran as fast as she could, the roar of the vehicle reminding her of another truck, and another time… Fear kept Kate on the run, and she flew over the five-foot smooth white fence at her pasture crossing, and kept her pace until she felt safe to slow down. Halfway across the pasture she slowed her heavy breaths and then relaxed, and fell into a even trot. Home was less than a mile away, and she could make that in easy stride. But then again the roaring, and the yelling, and the sound of crashing wood and medal, and the red truck came at her with speed. There was no place to hide in the open pasture, no barn, no crops of trees just wide open space. She zigzagged, made sudden quick stops and then reversed her direction it was both a thrilling challenge, and a run for her life…

There were two young men in the cab and two in standing in the bed of the truck, buckled to the crash-guards while they slung rope around in a wide circle yelling and laughing making background noise against the roaring truck. Kate ran, her tongue hanging out, panting, but then suddenly a weight landed around her head, and tightened…Kate went down, semi conscience as the truck finally slowed and the three of the young men were standing over Kate. One looked at the grinning driver. "What are trying to do kill us all!" He yelled and chucked the side of the pick-up hard with his boot. "Hey!" The driver yelled and cursed. 'I ought 'a drive off and leave your asses out here…" The roper stepped up close to the open window of the truck, and pulled a knife out of his back pocket and clicked the blade out. "Try it, *Mophead* and I'll mark-up that pretty face of yours!" "Take it easy Tex!" The second roper and the Shot-gun-rider yelled. "Are we taking this big ole sheep dog home, or letting her lie?" Shot-gun asked.

"He still breathing, Sid?" Tex asked, the other roper who was squatted behind Kate's head. "Yeah. It's a Bitch-dog. She's just passed out." Sid laughed. Just like a female, huh!"

"Well I wouldn't want to tangle with her when she wakes up...Toss me the muzzle, Thorn." Tex said to the driver with the wild head of dark curly hair. Tex caught the muzzle, but passed it on the Sid, who slipped it over Kate's head.

"Get the chain and the prod out of the truck-bed, Tag." Tex ordered the shot-gun rider.

"Let's just leave, her Tex, Tag said. Look, she's not a stray or some wild dog, she *belongs to someone...*"

"And how do you know that?" Tex said cynically.

"Heck it's obvious as tits on a cow! She's clean, even smells good, and she's well fed." Tag said. He stood with his hands in the back pockets of his levies, thumbs out. "I don't think she's dog fighting material, Tex."

"That so? We'll see!" Tex said as he gave the chain to Sid to put around Kate's neck in case she got free of the rope, keeping a safe distance. Tag laughed. "You scared, Tex?"

"Am I what?" Tex clicked the Switch-Blade and stuck it under Tag's nose.

"Uh, a real brave soldier.!" Tag exclaimed. And then mumbled, "When you got that knife"...after Tex had put it away. Thorn heard his younger brother's mumbled retort, and laughed.

"You two glamour boys get your royal be-hinds over here and help get this big rascal into the truck-bed!" Tex yelled. Kate woke up scrambled to her feet and set off running, unaware aware of which way and where she was going. "Hey, Hey, Hey!" Sid yelled hanging on the chain, but lost his footing and was dragged alone behind Kate. "Heeeelp!" Sid yelled. Tex hurriedly looped the rope around the crash-guard, and tied a tight knot, pulling back on it with all his strength. Thorn revved the engine. "Don't chase her dumb-butt!" Tex yelled. Kate suddenly came to the end of the long rope, lost her footing, and went air-born and landed hard. Sid landing across her flanks. Kate again lost air, and lay staring at the stars struggling for breath.

"Loosen the damned rope Sid!" Tag came running, and yelled for Tex to slack the rope. Sid groaned and stumbled to his feet. "Hell-of-a –ride – boys!" He grinned. Tag tossed the loop-end of the long rope to Sid. "Tie that to the chain and hurry before she wakes up!" Tag exclaimed.

"Gees, Tagger, a little more warning, next time…huh?" Sid said as he hastened to run the rope through the chain-links and secure it. Kate stood, muzzled, and held by rope and chain; a roaring growl whistling through her throat and out her nose and the space between the slight raise of her upper lip, her fangs glinting in the moonlight. Tex came with the prod….

21. CHAPTER TWENTY

Thorn Brookwell drove the speed limit up highway 95 to Dawson, while Kate was secured, standing in the back of the pick-up, muzzled, angry, and fearful; her white coat of hair flaring in the wind. Thorn and Tag Brookwell were the son's of the upstanding, and well respected Cattleman, and Volunteer Fireman, of Dawson. His home on the outskirts of Dawson had been in his family for three generations. It was not yet considered Historic, but highly noted as The Brookwell Mansion. Zeb Brookwell was an easy-going soul, who indulged his two sons. Their mother, Madge, would soon as take a strap to *them* as look at *them*, but Zeb always made a joke of their sons meanness, and found nothing amiss with the boys running with *that Sid Parks,* and worse, *that weird kid, Tex,...something or other!*

"There's your baby-boys, mother." Zeb said pointing his pipe stem at the red Ford pick-up truck passing by the house. "Guess we can go on back in the house and take supper out of the warmer." Zeb said. Madge had just stepped out on the porch, but Zeb had been sitting in the porch swing smoking his pipe and contemplating as he did most evenings. He secretly worried about his sons, wondering when they might start growing up and acting like *real men*...He'd never admit his concern to their mother, the woman worried enough for the both of them. But Zeb was considering taking some different strategies with his boys, but he hadn't got it all locked in as yet. "I'm hungry as a bear!" Zeb said rising up from the swing. He was a broad-built healthy fifty-two year old man, married to a natural red-head, ten years younger than him, who was once a Trick Rider and a Barrel Racer on her Palomino pony, Tracer, and won prize money and Blue Ribbons at the County and State Fairs - in her younger years. She was still slender, curvy, and a hand-full, but Zeb Brookwell wouldn't want her any different than she was.

"What was that they had in the back of the truck?" Madge asked.

"Well I'm not sure, but it sort of looked like a Sheltie Pony."

"Now what in the world would that Yahoo's of ours want with a Sheltie?" Madge exclaimed.

"Who knows?" Zeb shrugged, and opened the screen door and pressed his wife's lower back ushering her inside.

"Well we're sitting down to supper like *normal people*, you and I. The boys might have grabbed a burger on their way home." Madge said exasperated.

"Shoot, mother, they'd still be ready to eat your good cooking, you know it!" Zeb laughed. They sat down to a fine roast-beef dinner with all the trimmings.

"Thorn and Tag are up to something Zeb, and it is always something no good, and *you know it*." Madge spoke firmly unable to let the issue go, but she kept her voice level and on the quiet side.

"...Now mother..."

"Would you please stop calling me "mother," Zeb Brookwell. I am not *your* mother, but I'd rather be yours than those two outlaws of ours!"

"Oh come on Madge...Sweetheart...the boys are not so bad...just sowing..."

"Don't say it Zeb, don't you dare say it!"

"Ok, Ok, woman, just calm down, you're ruining my dinner!"

"I'm a good mind to kick Thorn and Tag out of the house... They're two years out of High School, and all they do is run around doing stupid stuff...Everybody in Dawson knows it, but they think so well of you...well folks don't want to mention anything against your sons."   "We'll come up with something moth...darling. I promise." Zeb smiled encouragingly.   "Indeed we will and I hope before they end up in prison!" Madge replied. Zeb laughed and asked Mage to pass the potatoes.

Ω

Tex and Sid had laid-low in the back of the truck when they passed the Brookwell home. The 'old man' was "cool" but the 'old lady' was so un-cool she could thaw the Arctic! Tex informed Sid when they had passed the house and sat up straight. "So she's to blame for Global Warming?" Sid joked, but Tex missed the connection, and looked quizzically at Sid.

"Are you planning to sell that big dog to Dewitt for the fights?" Sid asked nodding at Kate, whom he'd been watching. The canine girl looked proud and alert not broken or beaten, but Sid wondered how long she'd stay that way if left to Tex and Dewitt. They could make killers out of the most sublime canines, or break their spirit to pieces. Sid wasn't into the business of Dog Fighting it was just meeting up with his old friend, Tex, that put him on the edge of it.

Tex lit a slender cigarillo and puffed smoke. "I think she'd draw a crowd, being different from the usual breeds used in the business; Rottweiler's, Bull Dogs, and German Shep's, not ever a Sheepdog like this one." Tex flipped ash toward Kate, but Kate didn't move. She was short- chained close to the cab of the truck, but she could move her head to the left and right, slightly, and she was on her feet and could move a foot forward or backward. Kate was not in a position to fight or make threats, so she determined to keep her head for the right moment.

"I don't know Tex". Sid said shaking his head. "This dog is *different* – and I don't mean just her looks. She seems very intelligent...Didn't you notice how she gave us a good run, zigzagging, braking to a stop while we went flying by!" Sid laughed.

"She's a dog like any other dog, just bigger, that's all. It was Mophead's driving, that's all that gave *Harriet* there the advantage." Tex spat out the side of the truck.   "Guess we'll find out what she's made of..." Sid said, feeling a bit sorry for "Harriet".

The truck slowed as they approached Dewitt Krown 's backwoods barn. It was a large octopod-type building with a high roof that slanted at its eight sides, with fiber-glass shutters that opened and locked- closed hydraulically. Large ceiling fans dropped low over the wood-plank bleachers that lined four sides of the barn. In the middle of the big barn stood a tall metal ring bolted to the saw dusted floor. During the dogfights three men stood with guns at the ready in case one of the *killer's* got loose or out of control – or their owners. A fancy Mahogany Bar was set up in one corner and tended by "Professional" Bouncers and Biker Girls, most over thirty –five, some grandmothers, but wiry and tough looking. Outside armed Patrolmen were stationed in front of the barn, taking turn about to check-out the field that spread out on seven acres where trucks parked, and the Portable Potty, stood out back, practically hid by low-hanging branches of trees.

But there was no dogfights this weekday night, but the Bar was usually opened and some of the local Red-Necks gathered to sing and play a variety of styles of music – from Blue Grass to Country-Western to Old Rock, and even some of the famous old Gospel Songs, which nobody seem to object too and even got a bit misty-eyed over. It was a place some folks thought was just made-up out of some story-tellers imagination and other's "knowed" about it, but kept it to themselves. The County didn't interfere, because it was on private property, and they pretended that it just didn't exist.

    Dewitt Krown was sitting outside his establishment with two of his long-time cronies just "shooting the bull," as they called their conversations mixed realities, when the Brookwell brothers drove up in their two-year-old red Ford pick-up. Dewitt didn't mind the Brookwell un-look-a-like twins, or even Sid Parks, but he was in no mood for Tex Newman. He was a hot-head, and liked to snap that switchblade in a man's face to quick and too often. Tex regretted ever hiring the guy to clean-up around the place and other odd jobs. Tex had surely brought in two crowd pleasing Fighters, but now the kid thought he owned the place...He was getting complaints from clients and customers alike, and frankly Dewitt felt an unease about the guy.

    "Hi ya boys!" Dewitt greeted Thorn and Tag, and banged his fist lightly on the side of the truck. He looked up at Tex, ignoring

Sid who jumped over the tailgate to the ground. "What are you doing here Tex...Dewitt glanced at Kate standing statue in her fetters.

"Brought you a fighter, or she will be when I'm done training her." Tex said, and grinned. "You know I only use male dogs, Tex, and no Sheepdog male or female!" Dewitt grunted a laugh.

"What about Grey-Devil, he's a shepherd dog, right?"

"He's also German, that makes him eligible." Dewitt heaved a sigh. "Look I don't have to explain anything to you, boy. Just take this big piece of hair and get out of here!" Dewitt Krown turned and walked away, but Tex jumped upon the ridge of the truck bed, balanced there and yelled "Hey Krown!" Dewitt looked back to see Tex leap off the truck and land at his back. "What...the...heck! He spun around and Tex had his blade out and at the tip of Dewitt's chin. Dewitt was years older than Tex, but he was lean and hard muscled, and he'd been in plenty of fights in his time, and Vietnam taught him there was no such thing as a fair fight. Dewitt lifted a fist and knocked the knife out of Tex' hand, and raised a powerful knee kick at Tex' groin. The younger man went down screaming in pain, while the Brookwell boys gaped opened mouth at the quick turn of events. Sid came to his friend's aid. One of Dewitt's cronies stood and lifted a pointer-finger to deliver instruction: "Take him home, son, and set him in a hot tub of water, and dose him with a couple shots of whiskey. He'll be fine in a couple of days!"

"Yeah, thanks." Sid said as he helped Tex into the back of the truck. "Drop us off at my place in town, Sid told Thorn who had his head out the window to look at the fallen, and fallen at the hands - knee - of an old guy. Unbelievable! "Sure thing, Sid." Thorn called, and turned the Ford around .   Kate turned her head to look at the humankind who had lost the fight. Kate had watched it all, and was satisfied that her main enemy was taken down, yet she held some innate sympathy for the fallen. "What are you looking at Dog?" Tex yelled, and then doubled over in pain. Tex swore and cussed into his hat to hide his red eyes that were over-flowing water. Tex grabbed the prod and threw it hard into Kate's side, his anger providing the power for the hard thrust. Kate shook and withered with pain, the muzzle preventing anything but a whistle of audible pain as she dropped to the floor, the chain shortened to keep her standing, pulled the noose tight, and Kate struggled to her feet, leaning her weight against the cab of the truck.

"Are you happy now, Tex?" Sid jerked the black tattered Stetson from Tex' face. And stared in shock at the sorry-eyed, wet-faced hothead. "Do I look happy?" Tex croaked.

22. CHAPTER TWENTY ONE

Tag Brookwell had taken the restraints off Kate as soon as they dropped Tex off with Sid at Sid's apartment; a Victorian affair, of three stories plus the attic with screened sun porch and gables; painted in different l colors and with a fancy scalloped sign that read "Old House Apartments." The Brookwell twins didn't know on which floor Sid's apartment was located, but since Sid did not request their help they figured it must be on the first floor, and sped away quickly. Thorn stopped along Dawson Creek Bridge and Tag gingerly remove the muzzle, telling Kate he was sorry for *kidnapping* her, and for what Tex had done to her.

"Me and my brother, Thorn here, we're going to take care of you." Tag nodded toward Thorn, who kept a safe escape distance on the ground just in case the captured canine might seek revenge when released. But Kate was injured along her left flank, bruised and sore from all the forceful prodding, which Tex had abused her, and was not in any shape to run. Kate could sense the difference between bad, and stupid. Tag and Thorn were not bone-core bad, just a little spoiled and a whole lot stupid, but Kate never offered a grateful lick or even a weak smile of thanks, and seriously considered biting them both on their backend, perhaps she might –later, if given the chance.

"Sheltie, huh?" Madge gave her husband, Zeb a slightly disgusted look for all his playing-down their son's waywardness. She spoke with her hands cemented to her hips and green eyes blazing. "Zebadiah- Bernard- Blackwell: take this poor, sweet dog right down to Doctor Martin Fare, Madge exclaimed. I'll call him and tell him you're bringing in an emergency patient…he'll open up for you…And you boys stay right where you are, and don't you even blink!" Madge finished, before she slammed into the house to use the phone.

Thorn and Tag looked at their daddy for his usual light-hearted arbitration on their behalf, but Zeb only shrugged as if he didn't know what was on their momma's mind. The twins shared an equal amount fear in the look of exchange that passed between them. They'd better tread lightly and keep their mouths shut with Madge.

"Well go on, Zeb, the doc's on his way, Mage called from the porch at her husband. You boys come on in the house, I've got *news for you!*"

"Why are you so mad, Momma?" Thorn asked a little exasperated. "Tag and me didn't hurt that dog, we brought her home to take care of her." He explained.

"Is that right? Well tell me why Lula May Jackson called me up and said her sister in-law over in Gentry called her and said their pasture gate had been bashed in and somebody said there was a red pickup truck with a bunch of wild boys in it chasing a great big dog in their pasture, and tearing-up –jack!" Now does that sound familiar to you two Yahoos?" Madge demanded. Thorn and Tag dropped their head. They were caught, and no need denying it.

"Momma we're *real* sorry – and we mean it this time!" Tag said. "We'll swear it on a stack of Bible's won't we Thorn?" They faced their mother hopefully.

"Sure will Mom!" Thorn agreed. "It was Tex...he got us into this mess...it was all his idea..." Thorn saw his mother's face pinch up and then crunch in anger.

"Look, you boys are not dealing with your adoring father. The man's so proud of his son's he could bust, and can't see any wrong in anything you boys do. But I got eyes, and I love you enough to tell you both that you're not breaking that dear man's heart, and you aren't about to break mine!" "Now your Uncle David is coming to see us, and he's agreed to take you boys home with him to Ohio and put you to work, give you some training, and teach you how to be responsible young men...You give my brother any trouble and he'll fix you good, got it?"

"Yes ma'am!" Tag and Thorn exclaimed, their head hanging

again and their hands crunching up their ball caps. "Now you're daddy and I will pay the damaged you've done that we know about, and I'm reporting to the State Attorney's office about the illegal profiting from those dog fighting shows of Dewitt Krowns, so if you boys have been mixed up with any of that business you'd best be out of town..." Thorn and Tag raised their dark heads and looked wide-eyed at each other. They didn't think their *innocent* mother would know about such things, they both looked at her in awe.

"Well...uh...we just did a little clean-up...odd jobs for Dewitt...but Momma, Dewitt and Tex had a fight tonight, and the old guy sucker-punched...er.. knee-capped Tex in the privates, and 'bout killed him...old Dewitt will think it's Tex that's got the law out to his place...Well he might just kill Tex..." Tag explained.

"Then we best get Tex put in the jail as soon as possible for his own protection." Madge said, and sent her boys upstairs to pack, and to *'Think about what kind of men you want to be."*

Down at the Clinic Zeb waited and worried about Kate's condition, until he couldn't stand not knowing, and unsure if his boys were responsible for the big dogs injuries. He was alone in the waiting room; it was just him and Doc Fane, and the big canine. The lights were low in the waiting room, but bright as sun in the doctor's surgery room. Zeb quietly sneaked in. He looked at the big dog lying on the gurney still as death, her eyes staring. His heart seemed to flip-flop, as he worked the brim of his straw hat, held with both hands. "Is she dead, Doc?" He asked.

"No she's just sleeping. I've given her a mild sedative. This dog is in a lot of pain. She's bruised on her sides and flank, and I'm sure she has bruising on the inside along her flank where she took the worst punishment. I've got her on an IV with nutrients and pain meds. I will have to keep her in the Clinic a few days, Mr. Brookwell."

"Oh sure, do what you have to do, Doc; I'll take care of the bill."

"So you say your boys found this Komondor Sheepdog in this condition?"

"My boys didn't hurt the dog, as far as I know, but they were mixed up in the kidnapping."

"Kidnapping?" Doctor Martin Fane looked shocked.

"Oh, no sir..they…wouldn't…Dog-napping, they supplied the truck, and this one fellow, called Tex he did all the meanness to her." Zeb explained.

"I will have to report this to the authorities, Mr. Brookwell." Dr. Fane said.

"Sure, but my wife, she's done beat you to it."

"That's good." Doctor Fane smiled for the first time all evening. This Sheepdog is no stray, she's very healthy, and well cared for. I'm surprised she has no identifying collar or an implant…She is a very valuable canine…though she is not pure bred…I'd say that one of her parents is a Pon, a Polish lowland sheepdog. Their great sheep herders, but she has the full look of the Komondor, they are more like guardians. The doc added. This young lady is a beauty." The doctor concluded.

"Hey, that's what I am, Doc. Polish, but no dog, of course." Zeb chuckled lightly. She going to be all right, Doc?"

"I believe she will be just fine, but she needs medical attention…so you will be patient while I take good care of her, won't you?"

"No problem, Doc. Thank you so much for tending her…coming back to work…and all."

"That is nothing unusual for us Vet's, Mr. Brookwell." Doctor Fane smiled.

"Well then I must go, my wife is waiting at home, and anxious to know about the big dog."

"I am glad this one ended up with good people like you and your wife." The Doctor smiled and said good-evening Zebadiah Brookwell.

The following Monday the twins Uncle David Collins came to bring his nephews back to Ohio with him and put them to work in his vast Orchards. When he was done with them he was confident they would be ready for further education, University or Trade School, it didn't matter, but they would be begging him to send them to school somewhere, anywhere before the year was out. Tex Newman was picked up by a local County Officer, taken to the hospital, and afterwards put behind bars. Dewitt Krowns faced multiple charges for illegal profiting with canine fights, drugs and Alcohol, and numerous other infractions. He was out on Bond and made threats against Tex Newman. Sid Parks left town, and Tex was doing some serious thinking about his life while he awaited arraignment. He had a court appointed lawyer who looked like a wrestling champ. Tex would not be testing this guy. His switchblade had been confiscated.

Kate had been away from home for eight days. She was recovering well and kept in the Clinic's Kennel, but she was anxious to get back home. A notice was posted with the Gentry County Sheriff's office of a Komondor Sheep Dog thought to be missing from her Gentry Missouri home. When Greta heard from the Sheriff she knew it had to be Kate. She was on her way to Dawson after telling Flax and his boys they could stop looking, Kate had been found! Mattie was throwing her fresh baked rolls into the air in celebration, and Little Joe and Chloe were screeching their delight as they picked up fallen butter rolls in their chubby little hands and threw them at Mattie.

Kate was simply waiting for the opportunity to escape the Kennel and be on her way home to Greta, and Mattie, and Little Joe and Chloe. She missed the Robinson boys, and Flax as much, but in a different way; the longing to be with them, and the little bawling weaning calves was strong and unrelenting in Kate's heart and mind. She was obedient and friendly to the Kennel staff and they all loved Kate. The new employee, a young girl, called, Lilly, who loved *all animals*, adored Kate - and Kate was very fond of the girl –however; Kate's agenda was to find her way back home. Lilly sneaked extra treats for Kate, and played and talked with Kate as if she were her Mistress, and Kate built trust; staying when Lilly often left the kennel door closed, but unlocked and the door to the hallway open as she went about her duties. There was only one other canine in the recovery *room* of the Kennel with Kate. She was a large stately Poodle, who pranced around the tall metal pen as if it were a show room. Her name was Susie, and she liked Kate very much. They romped and played a little together, But Susie was a very picky eater, and she had not gotten her strength back, and tired easily. Kate nudged her to her bowl of special food prepared just for Susie, but Susie after a bite or two would walk away. Kate thought if she ate some of Susie's food it would surely infuse her appetite, but it did not. Susie, *they* said, was not eating enough to keep a bird alive. Kate worried. The next time Lilly brought Kate the illicit treats Kate pawed the bone-shaped treat towards Susie and Susie sniffed and played with it a while, but finally picked it up with her tongue and scoffed it down, and begged Kate for more. Kate buried the one she'd saved for later in Susie's food, and the tall, skinny Poodle ate her way to the treat, and from then-on Susie ate at least half her bowl of food, more in search of a treat than appetite, but the Kennel staff was pleased with Susie's progress.

The opportunity Kate had been waiting for happened on a rainy Wednesday morning. A pounding knock came at the rear door, where feed deliveries and employees usually came, and Lilly hastened to answer it. She left the Kennel door ajar in her haste while she opened the rear door to find Mr. Brookwell on the other side under a huge umbrella. He lifted his right hand as he smiled and waved a release statement in the air between them. "I've come to take the big Sheepdog home." He told Lilly. Just then the buzzer rang indicating Lilly was needed up front in the office.

"Excuse me, Mr. Brookwell, I'll be right back. She propped the door open for the transport of Kate, and waved Zeb Brookwell inside. Kate understood the buzzer meant Lilly was called up front so she pushed open the gapped Kennel cage door and hurried to the opened door to the hallway, which Lilly usually left open for her own convenience. Susie immediately followed, but Kate turned and gave Susie a low growl, and nodded her back. Susie tucked her tail and returned to the Kennel.

Kate recognized Zeb at the end of the hall, the large umbrella folded and held like a cane at his side. "Well, hey there, big-girl!" Zeb grinned. "That young lady just send you out?..."

Zeb looked at the release paper still in his hand and then at Kate. "We'd better wait a minute…I got 'a give that young lady this here notice of your release, you see." Zeb waved the paper in the air, as Kate suddenly bounded into a run and sped past him and out the door, while Zeb leaned as flat as he could against the wall to keep from being run over. When he recovered from the shock, Zeb banged on the door to the office, and when an angry looking office worker opened the door he tossed the Release form in the air. "The Sheepdog's gone, run out the back door. I've got to catch up with her!" He informed, as he rushed back down the hall.

    Kate in unfamiliar territory ran down the hill from the Animal Clinic, while men in trucks honked at the large white canine tearing down Main Street in pouring rain. Her breed was not a common one around Dawson, and the sight of her inspired Cell Phone photo's and video's of her. Kate began looking for a place to hide, and ducked down the first alleyway she came to. At the end of the alley she came upon a parking lot, partially filled with trucks, cars, and two-wheel vehicles. The noise of the honking horns, and the very cool soaking rain upset Kate, and caused her freshly healed wounds to throb so that the dilapidated rig, the color of wet sand, look inviting. It was dry inside and she was well hid behind the canvas flaps. There was even a blanket inside, and a plate with the scraps of someone's breakfast. Kate ate the strip of bacon, and licked the plate clean of egg yolk. She settled in to wait for the rain to slack, and to get her bearings. She didn't know that Greta Spangle clad in a yellow rain slicker and hat was stepping into the office of Doctor Martin Fane's Veterinarian Clinic at that very minute.

23. CHAPTER TWENTY TWO

Kate did not realize that her shelter was moving when she first awoke. It was the fast turn and the bump in the road that awakened and inspired Kate to poke her head out of the tent. The canvas flaps were dancing in the wind. The rain had stopped. The shelter had just turned off the Highway to a country road that smelled of wet dirt. The sun was cocooned in thick moisture, a blur of yellow, in the rain-sky. Kate felt defeated. She backed-up and lay back down a whimper escaping from way deep down inside her.

The moving Tent rumbled along. Kate did not know or care where it was going or how...She lay docile, and when at last it bumped and swayed to a stop, she did not move. She now smelled exhaust fumes, and the particular scent of the male human-kind. She heard the wind sway the branches of trees, and she head the ripple of a vast basin of water. She lay still. She would attack, even kill if she was attacked, but her warring defense melted away at the soft, cheerful whistling of the humankind. Kate's heart was struck with both joy and sorrow. The mouth-music sounded much like Joe Spangle's, the flaps of her shelter were suddenly thrown open, and a man stood in the opening his brown eyes wide with surprise. "Whoa!" He exclaimed, and backed away. There he stood. He did not move, Kate did not move, they simply stared at each other, eyes fastened by expeditious surprise.

"My name's Harrow. Adam Harrow" The humankind finally said. Uh, I got dry wood in the Cab and I'm about to fix some lunch...I don't mind sharing if you're interested?" Adam waited for some sort of response, but then said: "Whenever you're ready."

Shortly, Kate was tantalized by the smell of roasting meat

and some other spicy smelling protein, which put a sparkle in her eyes, and reason to risk a jump down from the shelter, which was not backed up to a dock as it was when Kate stepped into it. Her four paws did a little silent tap-dance, in anticipation of pain, because she knew now that her surgery was not completely healed. It had seemed so in the surgery kennel, with it's even ground and a soft bed, but the running exercise had proved differently. She gingerly stepped upon the back fender of the old beaten up- looking truck, and slid down the curve of it, which cut two or three feet from her jump. She shuffled toward the campfire where Adam held a thin rod with links of meat over the fire. Above in the tree hang a mirror, a security measure Adam Harrow took whenever he was alone at a campsite, a visual of what might come up behind him. He'd watched Kate's calculated descent from the truck, and the way she favored her left side, leaning her weight to her right side as she moseyed up to the campfire. She'd been injured for sure, but she looked very healthy otherwise. Some dog-owner must be on the look-out for this one, but until she was *found*, Adam didn't mind the company.

"Hot...dogs..." Adam began, then changed the vernacular, "Wieners on a bun, cheapest meal in any State!" You like chili?" Adam asked nodding to the pan sitting on hot ambers. "Might give you heartburn," Adam said and fisted his chest with a small thump, which produced a burp, but it's worth it." He said and shook a wiener onto a pie-tin and poured chili on the side. Kate devoured the wiener, but left the chili alone, and was fed another link of meat. At a closer look Adam noticed the patch of skin with recent surgical stitching, when the breeze lifted the longer hair of Kate's outer coat. "So you've been worked over and worked on... sort of like me." Adam gave a grunt of a chuckle. "At least we have something in common, you and me." Kate lay on her right side and gazed up at the man. He had a long dark 'tail' at the back of his head, and a shaggy beard that covered his chin. He was neither young nor old, and Kate sensed that he was the wondering kind, but she liked Adam Harrow. Kate spent one year with Adam Harrow, circling the southwestern part of the state, in the old brown flat-bed truck with the sand-color tent they both shared and survived the winter in with battery heated sleeping bags, but always returning to Dawson, where Adam had unfinished business.

'You've been a real true friend, Hairball, but there's no room for you in our little apartment... Yeah, my wife's taking me back, and I'm going to be good to her from now on. She's a good person, and she loves me too..." Adam explained. "There's a farm over yonder, and I know they are good folk, you head on over there", Adam said pointing, then fell upon Hairball's neck and wept. Kate watched as Adam and the old truck left her beside the road a few miles from Dawson's City Limit, the tent flattened and folded away, the truck sent through the Carwash back down the Highway. Adam had stayed in a motel cabin the previous night, making a sneaking invitation to "Hairball" to join him inside, but Kate preferred the outdoors, and slept on the grass in front of the little cabin. She sensed change in the air, and Adam appeared changed when he came out of the cabin the next morning, neatly shaved, and dressed, with a new determination in his brown eyes. Kate crossed the road, as Adam's old truck dimmed in the distance, passing vehicles honking warnings at her. She was unsure of her bearing, her memories of her past faded into obscurity and her present without plan or foundation as she made her wonderings alone Eastward.

She had lived on the edges of civilization, preferring the woods, the hunt for food, and the sky above. She traveled with a small pack of canine for a short while, fought with menace Coyotes, snakes, and some of her own kind; and was shot at, and missed, by humankind with their guns for her trespass. Good hearted farmers would leave food and fresh water for her in their pastures, but Kate belonged to no one, and hardly trusted anyone or anything; however, the kindness of farmers kept her heart tender towards man. And it was Kenny Evans that caught her attention in her seventh year. She had spent an apopemptic life, leaving and being left, and had finally come to a place of compromise with Kenny and Angel Evans. They let her be who she was, and she'd found her heart again with them. And now the glow of youth gone, her bones brittle with age she had come to remember the years before, and found the place where her heart was lost.

Little Sammy had gone with her again to that *particular* place leaving Digger behind with farewells. It was cold, but the snow on the ground was soft and only a few inches deep., and little Sammy hurried to his place of buried treasure where he'd been digging when the cry of the Bobcat sacred him, Katie Love, and Digger away, before he'd finished his purpose.   It was just two days later, and Katie had come looking for Little Sammy. She wanted to return to the place of the royal blue metal pieces, which Katie Love recognized as parts of Joe Spangle's Cessna. They were there now, and Sammy scratched away at the moist earth, while Katie licked the snow off the hollow rounded pieces of light covers and the small, royal blue chunks of wing of Joe's Cessna. Sammy barked as he pulled at the treasure still partially buried in the ground, that had Katie's scent, and the scent of a humankind, little Sammy did not recognize.   Katie looked up curious, and hurried to help Little Sammy retrieve his treasure. They dug until the ground released a dirty, tattered leather jacket. Katie had immediately gotten Joe scent from it, and gathered it beneath her body.   Katie gave a long mournful howl into the sky, and little Sammy scuttled away and stood gazing on his friend, a sympathetic whimper crackling in the cold winter wind. The snow began to fall steadily, and little Sammy urged Katie to follow him home Kate rose and dragged the jacket beneath the pine tree and covered it with pine branches while little Sammy ran to and fro in his eagerness for home. When Katie turned to follow, little Sammy ran ahead, and never looked back at the sudden screeching cry.

24. CHAPTER TWENTY THREE

Conroy Jarvis and his son, Scott drove up the narrow path into the wooded area on the east side of the property to fell a small pine tree for firewood. Conroy carried the power saw and Scott his hunting rifle. "Over there, son. That little tree by the pile of snow Conroy Jarvis said pointing. Scott who kept his eyes roving looked where his father pointed.

"That's not a snow pile Pop, it's a big ole'sheepdog. Scott whistled loud. "It's dead. Probably froze to death". The two men walked close. "Poor thing." Conroy said shaking his head, when his eye caught a glimpse of something else. "That gun of yours loaded, son?" Conroy asked low.

"You know it is" Scott said. "Have you spotted another *snow pile, Pop?*"

"Over there in the brushes, funny-boy, another dead animal I think. It's not moving." Conroy Jarvis said. Scott stooped and picked up a round piece of metal and threw it hard into the bush, the big cat staggered out screeching.

"Shoot!" Conroy yelled, and the powerful rifle was fired, its bullet hit the injured Bobcat between the eyes.

$$\Omega$$

Eight miles away Angel and Kenny Evans, bundled against the cold, stood on the porch, their eyes searching for Katie Love, while Jack and Annie were let out for morning *business*. Young Annie didn't seem to mind the cold, romping in the snow, but Jack was back on the porch ready for the warm indoors when they were all startled by the echoing sound of gunfire that seem to crackle in the snowy atmosphere.

"Goodness, that' shot must be heard around the world'!" Angel said as they all filed into the warmth of the house.

"Ken, I hope that wasn't somebody shooting at Katie Love

for trespassing...She's been gone for three days...free-ranging." Angel said when they were inside.

"Nobody around our community would shoot at a dog, Angel – not unless it was aggressive and out of control, and that's not our Katie. More likely it was a shot to drive off some pesky Coyote." Kenny said.

"But three days in this cold..." Angel worried.

"Katie is part working -dog, part street-dog, and part free-ranger, she knows how to take care of herself..." Kenny said to reassure himself as much as Angel. *But mostly just one big old dog with a big heart...*He said to himself, for if he said it out loud, he knew Angel would cry, and afraid that he would also.

It was a fretful day, not overt, but just knowing and not knowing or practically convinced, but in denial. Angel had set up her ensile at the dining room window to capture the front yard in its winter splendor and to keep her mind occupied, but palette and brush were dumped aside, and baking begun, when she could not keep her eyes off the empty Tent, the wind blowing the old camping comforter into the back of the shelter. Kenny found a summer counter fan to take apart and put back together. His real work was out in the barn, but it was too cold to work out there, and not as much enjoyed without....but the aroma of the baking cherry pie seem to fill the house with hope as well as its wafting flavor.

They were enjoying a second piece of pie and decaf while they watched the late news, and were drawn into a feature story about a farmer and his son killing a Bobcat in a wooded area of their property in the Elm Tree Community of Licking, Missouri. It happened early this morning, the Newscast Anchorman reported, when Conroy Jarvis and his son, Scott, set out to cut firewood. The big cat, injured from an apparent fight with a large Komondor Sheepdog, found dead, nearby, was shot when it came at the two men aggressively. The local Veterinarian said the big Cat would have died due to its injuries from the fight with the large Canine... The bobcat is not native to the area..."

"That was the shot we heard this morning." Angel said.

Katie was attacked by that Bobcat and killed." Her voice broke and she cried.

"Must be." Kenny agreed and he held his wife and they wept together.

Katie was transported, by Conroy Jarvis, and Scott Jarvis to the gravesite on the Evans' property, and buried next to Sugar, another sweet canine member of their family. Katie Love's homecoming was bitter-sweet. The bitter was the big feline that killed her, and her innate stubbornness that refused the care and protection her Mistress and Master so desired to give to her. The sweet was the loving time they shared with her, for the last six years of her life: And the letters they received from so many people that said Katie had passed through their life with blessings: Must have been our *"Kate"* our *"little girl"* lost long ago. "She sounds like *Hairball,* an awesome dog! And she fits the description of a sweet dog called *"Harriet"* that ran away from the Dawson kennel eight years ago! Flax Robinson, and his three sons, Toby, Billy and Tad E-Mailed that Katie, was Kate, the Komondor Sheepdog they worked with when she was just a pup. The staff at the Martin Air Station just outside of Branson, said that Katie Love had to be *Joe Spangle's co-pilot. And in a lovely sympathy card, a note:"* Greta *felt in her heart it had to be dear "Kate" a beloved family friend…"*

"My how many lives you've touched, Katie Love!" Angel said softly as she laid a pink rose on Katie's grave. "There will never be another Katie Love." Kenny said as he and Angel walked to the car, followed by Labrador Jack and his little Spaniel sister, Annie Marie.

Ω

THE END

About The Author

I was 6 months old when the Japanese bombed Pearl Harbor.

Two brothers of my mother; Amos and Kenneth Kennedy, volunteered to serve in the Army. My grandmother Kennedy, my mother Louis, and Aunt Elsie volunteered to work at the ammunition base and other "Government Girls" jobs that supported our Troops. I am one of six siblings of my mother, five of my father and mother. Dad was a house builder but preferred house painting and wallpapering. He loved to play his guitar and sing. My Aunts say that he was a rather handsome man and charmed, not only my mother with his singing and strumming but was a popular young guy around town. He had only one sibling, a young brother, and his mother came from a large family of eight siblings, five girls and three boys. All were raised in the Christian Faith, which was passed on to their children. The decision to embrace the Christian Faith is an individual decision and was never forced; but practiced in our home, church, and community.

My mother, Louis Cynthia Kennedy was a very lovely, quiet woman. She was wise and strong and died too young. At the age of 34, she left behind her daughter from her first marriage and us five Johnson kids that went from my secure loving environment to a new town. The adventures from Oklahoma to California and back after almost 10 years were sometimes close to normal. When they were not dramatic, we all survived the war of childhood but not without emotional scars. But we all had a sense of Faith and a sense of humor I may.

I was impressed with my Sacramento Aunt, a pretty redhead. Her personal time was spent lounging in bed with "My True Story" Magazines and a supply of Hershey chocolate bars kept in her bedside table drawer. I was seven years old but I had a great desire to read those magazines and kept asking to have them when she finished reading them. They were not reading material for children; my aunt informed me. But I begged and finally got what I wanted. She did not think I could read them or understand the content.

So, she relented and kept me supplied. I didn't understand a lot and some words were beyond my capacity, but basically, the stories were simply written. My dad soon put a stop to my reading material but he never replaced anything with "age-appropriate" reading. I then took up drawing and entered art instruction ads from the pages. I took out the "True Story Magazines" before Dad trashed them and threatened me with a whipping if I dared rescue them from the trash. I used up his writing tablet. Drawing pictures of animals' heads and grown-up women's heads and sometimes an automobile. I mailed them to the address in the ad. But they wrote back and said they were sorry, but my drawings did not indicate that I had an aptitude for drawing. With that and when Dad said I left him no writing paper for his own use, my drawing career ended. He promised to buy me a "Big Chief" tablet when he got paid for his current project.

The summer seemed endless in California, being bored and hungry. I would climb up on the porch railing of the wrap-around porch of the old house, then on the porch post and lean out and pick figs off the little tree, that stood up against the porch. There were outbuildings and shade trees that hung over the metal roof of the old chicken co-op. That was my brother's club "No Girls Aloud!" Further away down the old stickery patch, and remnants of mostly dead grass from an old garden patch were tiny chards of broken mason jars scattered about. Mason jars which someone used for canning jars were stashed beneath the house's open cellar, and even in every broken down outbuilding nearby.

The three small apricot trees out through the stickers and charred glass, were loaded down with delicious fruit every year. But still made us kids yearn for our neighbors, large sweet yellow peaches in their backyard orchard......and that is a story for another time.

Back home in Oklahoma at age sixteen, I read my first novel; Irving Stone's "Immortal Wife." My aunt Dorothy, who was about 8 years older than me, introduced me to novels. It was a fascinating reading about real people from a long time ago. Irving Stone novels were based on true historical facts, which I thoroughly enjoyed.

My education with all its interruptions is made up of my completion of high school equivalency. I attended Oklahoma State Technical College where I studied secretarial management and marketing. I attended various College courses in Oklahoma and Missouri. I attended Drury College in Springfield Missouri. My highest grades were in Creative Writing and Business Law at Oklahoma State Technical College, and at Drury College; I excelled in creative writing and sociology.

I have five wonderful children, 10 grandchildren, 18 great-grandchildren,

and 7 great-great-grandchildren. I know it's a miracle, but it's true. I am so blessed to see my grandchildren having much success in their marriages, and parenting with security and true love; all required ingredients to produce happy adults, and secure happy children- all of which are doing wonderfully well!

Sincerely,

Lee Kennedy-Johnson

Made in the USA
Coppell, TX
01 November 2023